Psychology and Education

Karen Legge
Philippe Harari

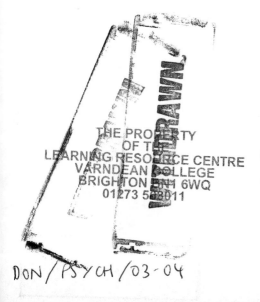

Psychology and Education

Karen Legge
Philippe Harari

Heinemann Educational Publishers
Halley Court, Jordon Hill, Oxford, OX2 8EJ
a division of Reed Educational & Professional Publishing Ltd

OXFORD MELBOURNE AUKLAND
JOHANNESBURG BLANTYRE GABORONE
IBADAN PORTSMOUTH NH(USA) CHICAGO

04 03 02 01
9 8 7 6 5 4 3

British Library Cataloguing in Publication Data
A catalogue record for this book is available from the British Library

ISBN 0 435 806556

Typeset by Wyvern 21 Ltd
Printed and bound in Great Britain by The Bath Press Ltd, Bath

Acknowledgements
The authors and publishers would like to thank the following for the use of copyright material: *The Guardian* for the article on p. 14; Macmillan Press Ltd for the extracts from *Psychology for Teachers*, Fontana, 1995 on pp. 49–50.

Cover photograph by: AKG London

The publishers would like to thank the following for permission to use photographs: Albert Bandura, Stanford University on pp. 7 and 9; Brandeis University on p. 23; Jerome Bruner on p. 31; Corbis on pp. 2, 4, 10, 15 (right), 29 and 32; Hulton Getty on pp. 1 and 17; Michael Newman, Summerhill School on p. 15 (left); R. Sommer on p. 55.

The publishers have made every effort to trace the copyright holders, but if they have inadvertently overlooked any, they will be pleased to make the necessary arrangements at the first opportunity.

Tel: 01865 888058 www.heinemann.co.uk

C Contents

Psychology and education

1 Introduction

Education is never neutral; it either oppresses or it liberates. Paulo Freire

Everything teachers do in the classroom reflects their personal beliefs – from the way they choose to lay out students' desks to how they deal with disruptive children. Although teachers may claim to be 'value-free' or neutral in the classroom, and try very hard to keep their personal opinions to themselves in order not to influence their students, in practice this is not possible. We believe that teachers should openly express beliefs in the classroom, either directly or in the way they behave, but that it should be made clear to students that these are merely beliefs. Using a position of authority to express beliefs and claim that they are 'facts' is oppressive. Helping students to evaluate and criticize other people's beliefs is liberating.

Teachers' beliefs about education arise out of their personal experience, their own education, the books they have read and so on. These beliefs cover a wide range of questions related to education, from determining the most effective way of imparting knowledge and skills to students to deciding how teachers should manage the classroom situation. Perhaps the most important question of all is about the fundamental purpose of education: is it to train people to do specific jobs, to create good citizens, or to lead people to intellectual or spiritual enlightenment? The role of educational psychology is to examine beliefs about learning and to support or criticize them on the basis of evidence and experience.

Chapter 1

This chapter describes two fundamentally different approaches to education: one based on behaviourist theory (classical and operant conditioning, and social learning) and the other on humanist theory (Carl Rogers' concept of student-centred learning). It also examines the cognitive approach to education, and focuses on the theories of Piaget and Vygotsky. Finally, the role of metacognition in education is discussed, using the recently introduced post-16 Key Skills as an illustration.

Chapter 2

The aim here is to show how the behaviourist, humanist and cognitive approaches are linked to the way teachers teach and assess learning. The first section examines assumptions about children's motivation to learn, and how this can be improved. In the second section, the work of three psychologists – Gagné, Bruner and Ausubel – and the implications of their ideas for teaching and learning are described. The chapter ends with a discussion of the purpose and effectiveness of different forms of educational assessment.

Chapter 3

This chapter is about managing the classroom, both in terms of dealing with behavioural problems and with the physical classroom environment. It describes the different types of behavioural problems that may be encountered in a classroom, and the variety of techniques for dealing with them. This relates closely to Chapter 1, as classroom management techniques can be linked to the different theoretical perspectives.

Chapter 4

This chapter describes how gender, ethnicity and class affect learning, then goes on to examine a number of explanations of why this happens. The final two sections consider different types of special needs (including giftedness) and discuss ways of meeting them in the classroom. In particular, arguments are set out in favour of and against integrating children with special needs into main-stream classrooms.

How to use this book

This book has a number of features to help you understand the topic more easily. It is written to give you a wide range of skills in preparation for any of the new AS and A level psychology syllabi. Opposite is a list of the features with a brief summary to explain how to use them.

1 Real Life Applications

These consist of 'text boxes' that develop further a concept already discussed within the main text. Often they provide articles or outlines of studies. In all cases they attempt to apply theory to 'real life situations'.

2 Commentary

These paragraphs appear throughout the book. They follow on from issues raised within the main text. They serve a number of functions: to provide an evaluation of the earlier text, to clarify a point or to highlight some related issue. Sometimes they provide 'for' and 'against' debates.

3 Key studies

As the title implies these are descriptions of important studies within a specific area. There are two of these for each chapter. They briefly identify the aims, method, results and conclusions of the study. This feature helps you to understand the methodology of research.

4 Questions

Each 'Real Life Application' has two or three short answer questions designed to test a range of skills including summarising, outlining and evaluating. All of these activities are designed to allow you to acquire the 'study skills' outlined within the syllabi. In addition, two or three 'essay-style' questions are included at the end of each chapter. They relate specifically to the material covered within the chapter.

5 Advice on answering questions

There is a short section at the end of this book that gives brief advice on answering all the essay questions. It also provides answers to the short questions presented in this book.

1 Theoretical perspectives

This chapter describes two fundamentally different approaches to education: one based on behaviourist theory and the other on humanist theory. It also examines the cognitive approach to education. Finally, the role of metacognition in education is discussed, using the recently introduced post-16 Key Skills as an illustration. Real Life Applications that are considered are:

* RLA 1: Token economies
* RLA 2: Summerhill School
* RLA 3: Key Skills in Curriculum 2000.

Early psychologists often studied mental processes using a process of **introspection**, looking inside their own minds to describe and analyse their conscious experience. However, at the beginning of the twentieth century **behaviourist** psychologists began to criticize the idea that psychology was about the study of inner consciousness.

The behaviourist approach

Behaviourists disapproved of introspection on the grounds that it was subjective and could not be replicated; they accepted that the mind existed, but argued that it was impossible to observe it scientifically. Behaviour, on the other hand, could be observed and was therefore considered the only legitimate subject matter for scientific psychology. Traditional behaviourists are not interested in what is going on in people's minds. Instead, they try to establish laws that link environmental stimuli with specific actions; their aim is to describe, predict and control behaviour.

Behaviourists believe that organisms behave in particular ways as a result of adapting to their environment; behavioural adaptation is learnt by making **associations**. In this section, we will describe three different ways in which people learn behaviour through the process of association: **classical conditioning, operant conditioning** and **observational learning**. We will also discuss the implications of these three theories for education.

Classical conditioning

Ivan Pavlov, a physiologist and Nobel Prize-winner who became well known for his use of dogs in experiments on classical conditioning.

Ivan Pavlov (1849–1936) was a physiologist who, in 1904, won the Nobel Prize for his research into digestion. As part of his work, he designed a special device that he fitted into the mouths of laboratory dogs in order to collect their saliva. Animals salivate when they are presented with food, and this automatic response has the function of aiding digestion. Pavlov noticed that his dogs would salivate before the food came – for example, when the experimenter came into the room and turned on the light. He concluded that the dogs had made an association between the light being turned on and the food arriving. As a result, he could get the dogs to salivate simply by turning on the light, even if there was no food present at all. The dogs had adapted to their environment by learning an automatic **response** (that is, salivation) to a particular **stimulus** (that is, the light). He called this process classical conditioning.

Pavlov argued that the learnt association between the stimulus and the response was temporary and that if, for example, he continued to put on the light without presenting his dogs with any food, they would eventually stop salivating. This is called **extinction**. He also pointed out that, following a traumatic experience, the stimulus–response bond could be learnt very quickly, sometimes after only one trial. He noticed this when his dogs almost drowned after their kennels flooded; as a result of this single experience, many of them became afraid of water. This is called one-trial learning, and extinction seems to take longer in such cases.

John Watson, along with Rosalie Rayner, proved that classical conditioning could also be applied to human beings.

In 1920, John Watson (a major figure in behaviourism) and Rosalie Rayner carried out the first experiment to show that classical conditioning could be applied to human beings as well as other animals.

KEY STUDY 1

Researchers: Watson and Rayner (1920)

Aim: To show that an emotional response (that is, fear) to a neutral stimulus (that is, a pet white rat) can be conditioned in a human being.

Method and results: This was a case study carried out on a single participant, a young boy known as 'Little Albert'. There is always a problem in generalising from a single case, but Watson was trying to demonstrate the existence of a particular phenomenon (that is, classical conditioning in humans). In order to do so, he only had to find one example. After gaining consent from his mother, Albert (aged nine months) was presented with a white rat and showed no fear of it whatsoever. When Albert was eleven months, Watson and Rayner began the conditioning process. They presented the rat to Albert and, at the same time, struck a steel bar with a hammer immediately behind the child's head in order to frighten him. A week later, they showed the rat to Albert without banging the steel bar; he whimpered, cried and fell over. After another week, they presented Albert with a rabbit and he exhibited the same fear reaction as for the rat. He was also frightened of a dog (but slightly less so), a fur coat, some cotton wool and a Santa Claus mask. Over the next few days, Albert's fear reactions began to die out, but were brought up to the same levels again by banging the steel bar behind his head at the same time as he saw the rat. A month later, Albert still cried when shown the Santa Claus mask.

Conclusions: Watson and Rayner felt that their study showed that it was possible to condition emotional responses in human beings. Although these responses grew weaker over time (extinction), they were still present a month later. In fact, Watson and Rayner stated that these learned associations would persist throughout the rest of Albert's life and continue to affect his behaviour (which, if true, does raise an important **ethical** issue).

Implications of classical conditioning

The implications of classical conditioning for teaching are less important than those of two other behaviourist theories (described in the text that follows), but there is a need for teachers to try to make sure that students associate only pleasant emotional responses with educational situations. For example, classical conditioning may explain why some children develop school phobia.

If a student is bullied at school, then they may learn to associate school with fear (see Figure 1, below). This learnt response could persist after the bullies have stopped, or even if the child moves to another school. A student may develop a seemingly irrational dislike of a particular subject that continues throughout his or her school career following an unpleasant experience – such as a teacher humiliating him/her in front of the class. It is not unusual for teachers to punish students – for example, by giving them extra work to do, staying behind in detention and writing an essay. If this happens several times, the student may associate writing essays with the negative emotions s/he feels as a result of receiving the punishment.

The implication is that schools should be happy places in which children experience positive emotions. This means that, as far as possible, teachers should avoid punishment, though punishment is an important component of the second behaviourist theory, operant conditioning.

Commentary

There are several evaluation points to be made about the theory of classical conditioning, as follows.

- It is a **scientific** theory, because it is based on empirical observation carried out in controlled experiments.
- It adopts an **environmentalist** view of human nature – that is, it assumes that most, if not all, human behaviour is learnt through interacting with the environment, and not inherited.
- Following on from the last point, it is **egalitarian** in that it assumes that people are born the same as each other; what makes us different in terms of personality is the different stimulus–response associations we learn.
- It is **determinist** in that it does not allow for any degree of self-determination in the individual. We have no control over the reactions we have learnt through classical conditioning; in theory, all human behaviour could be predicted.
- It is **reductionist** in that it reduces organisms to machines that are constantly being programmed and re-programmed; it suggests that much of our behaviour has a single cause.

Operant conditioning

Behaviourist psychologists who followed Watson recognized that his ideas were too reductionist to be a complete explanation of human behaviour; they

	Pavlov's dogs	Little Albert	School phobia
Stage 1: before conditioning	Light → No response Food → Salivating	Rat → No response Loud noise → Fear	School → No response Bullying → Fear
Stage 2: during conditioning	Light ⎫ Food ⎭ → Salivating	Rat ⎫ Loud noise ⎭ → Fear	School ⎫ Bullying ⎭ → Fear
Stage 3: after conditioning	Light → Salivating	Rat → Fear	School → Fear

Figure 1: Examples of classical conditioning

could not deny that human beings sometimes *decided* to behave in certain ways. Whereas classical conditioning is concerned with respondents (that is, involuntary reactions elicited by stimuli), operant conditioning is concerned with operants (that is, instrumental acts that have an effect on the environment). For example, salivating or fear are respondents, whereas picking up a pencil is an operant.

Edward Lee Thorndike (1874–1949) carried out many experiments in which he placed various animals in 'puzzle boxes'. For example, he would put a cat in a cage, then encourage the cat to escape using a piece of fish. The cat could escape, but only after carrying out three specific actions, such as lifting a lever and so on. At first, the cats would try to scratch at the bars in an ineffectual way. Eventually, by chance, they would hit upon the right sequence of moves and escape from the cage. When put back in the cage, it would take them much less time to escape a second time. Thorndike argued that the cats had made an association between an operant (that is, the specific actions needed to open the cage door) and a reward (that is, the piece of fish); they had learnt by 'trial and error'.

The psychologist BF Skinner developed the work of Thorndike to form his own theory of operant conditioning.

BF Skinner (1904–1990), one of the twentieth century's most influential psychologists, developed Thorndike's ideas into the theory of operant conditioning. He argued that behaviour is learnt through a process of trial and error; if a particular behaviour is systematically rewarded, then we will repeat it; if it is punished, then we will avoid it. He carried out experiments on rats in a 'Skinner Box'. This apparatus consisted of a cage with a small lever that the rat could press. Skinner could train the rats to press the lever repeatedly by rewarding them with a pellet of food every time they did so; alternatively, he could train them to avoid the lever by punishing them with a mild electric shock when they touched it.

In educational settings, there are various types of **reinforcers** (or rewards) that can be used to encourage children to behave in particular ways. First, reinforcement can be **extrinsic** or **intrinsic**.

Extrinsic reinforcement is presented to an individual by other people – either deliberately (for example, by offering a child a financial reward to do a chore) or inadvertently (talking to a child when s/he misbehaves without realizing that you are actually rewarding the child with the attention s/he craves). Intrinsic reinforcement, on the other hand, comes from within the individual and may consist of, for example, the feeling of satisfaction a student may have when s/he hands in work on time and thereby feels in control of his/her own studies. Behaviourists tend to focus on extrinsic reinforcement, because this can be manipulated in order to change other people's behaviour.

Second, reinforcement can be **social** or **material**. Social reinforcement in the classroom would include the praise and approval of the teacher, or even just being given more attention; these may be given directly to students (for example, the teacher saying 'Well done'), or by using signs such as ticks, gold stars and so on. Material reinforcement consists of more concrete rewards – such as sweets or money, being allowed to play a computer game or being given *tokens* that can be cashed in at a later date for a material reward.

Finally, reinforcement can be **positive** or **negative**. The examples given in the previous paragraph are all positive reinforcement because they consist of giving the child something that s/he values (that is, a reward). The other way to reinforce behaviour is to remove punishment or the threat of punishment (that is, a **relief**). For example, allowing a child to leave detention early because s/he has been good is a negative reinforcement; the child is not being offered an actual reward, but the punishment s/he expected to receive is being withdrawn.

As well as reinforcing certain 'good' behaviour, the teacher can also discourage children from acting in ways that s/he disapproves of by punishing 'bad' behaviour. Punishment can consist of taking away rewards (that is, **penalty**). Examples in the classroom include putting students in detention (taking away their break time) or preventing students taking part in an enjoyable activity because they have misbehaved. Punishment can also involve imposing something unpleasant on the student. Types of punishment used in schools include the following.

- **Reprimands:** these can range from being shouted at by a teacher in front of the class to a look of mild disapproval.
- **Exclusion:** children can be made to sit in a corner or on a table by themselves, asked to stand outside the door or sent to a special supervized room. At a school wide level, students can be temporarily suspended or permanently expelled. This may involve the student in having to attend another school, or maybe a special unit for children with behavioural difficulties.
- **Unpleasant activities:** teachers give children extra work or lines to write, make them pick up litter or clean desks and so on.
- **Withdrawal of benefits:** some schools have point systems and students can be 'fined' for misbehaving. Also, students can have their break times withdrawn (detention) or be stopped from taking part in pleasurable activities.
- **Corporal punishment:** shaking or hitting children is now against the law in schools in the UK, but it used to be fairly commonplace.

For a full discussion of the effectiveness of punishment and of the ethical questions it raises, see the text on behaviourist approaches to classroom management (page 44).

Establishing a schedule of reinforcement
Once a teacher has decided that s/he wishes to change the behaviour of his/her students using operant conditioning techniques, s/he has to establish a **schedule of reinforcement**. For example, **continuous reinforcement** means that a reward is given every single time the child exhibits the 'correct' response. This has the advantage that the child will learn very quickly to behave in a particular way. However, the fast rate of learning is balanced out by a fast rate of extinction; when the rewards are stopped, then the child very quickly ends the behaviour.

An alternative technique is **partial reinforcement**; in this, the rewards are not given every single time, but maybe every other time or every third time, or even at random intervals in response to the correct behaviour. With this schedule, the rate of learning is much slower, but so is the rate of extinction; because the child has not got used to receiving a reward every time, when the rewards stop, s/he perseveres with the behaviour in the hope that the reward will eventually come. An example of how partial reinforcement can be harmful is when a child is nagging to be allowed to do something (play with the computer, for example). If the teacher starts by refusing permission, but eventually gives in to the child's persistence, the child learns that nagging is a successful strategy and will persevere next time, even after the teacher repeatedly says 'No'. It would be better for the teacher to agree to the child's request immediately or, having refused, stick to this decision.

In practice, formal reinforcement schedules often use a combination of continuous and partial reinforcement, by starting with rewarding every correct behaviour so that learning takes place quickly, then expecting more and more instances of the behaviour before offering the reward so that the child comes to depend less on the reinforcement.

Commentary

- The text below compares different types of reinforcement.
  - Intrinsic versus extrinsic: there may be situations in which the intrinsic benefits of a behaviour are not immediately apparent, and extrinsic reinforcement is needed in order to get the child to behave in a particular way, at least to begin with. However, if that behaviour has no intrinsic reward at all, then the behaviour is likely to stop very quickly once the extrinsic rewards are withdrawn (extinction). For example, if you bribe children with money in order to get them to do their homework, they are much more likely to continue doing their homework if they also receive a sense of internal satisfaction from it. (A more detailed comparison of extrinsic and intrinsic reinforcement is described on page 23 on motivating students.)
  - Social versus material: it may seem that material rewards, such as money or toys, would be more valued by children than social rewards such as

approval, and would therefore be more effective in modifying behaviour. However, social reinforcement is commonly used in classrooms, and there is a great deal of evidence to indicate that it is, in fact, more effective than offering material rewards. Hall (1989) suggests that material rewards only work because of the social reinforcement that is given at the same time. In a **token economy**, for example, tokens are given to children in order to reward them for specific actions (see RLA 1 opposite). These tokens can be cashed in for material rewards. However, if the teacher says 'Well done' as s/he hands over the token, then the child is also receiving social reinforcement and it is this, rather than the token itself, that may be motivating behavioural change.

  – Positive versus negative: the disadvantage of using negative reinforcement is that it has to be linked to some kind of punishment, which can then be removed in order to reward the child. Apart from the negative implications of using punishment in the first place (see page 45), negative reinforcement can have the effect of teaching children to avoid or escape from unpleasant situations. Clearly, avoiding an unpleasant situation is sometimes the best course of action, but this is not always the case and it would be a mistake to encourage children to be avoidant by over-using negative reinforcement.

• It is very important for teachers to be consistent in the way they reinforce behaviour. Students who are faced with moody and unpredictable teachers become confused about which behaviours get rewarded and which get punished. One reaction to this is for the students to become sullen and passive, reluctant to make contributions to lessons in case they get into trouble. Another way in which teachers can misuse reinforcement is to punish one student for the actions of another. Haney, Banks and Zimbardo (1973), in their simulated prison study, describe **arbitrary control** as one of the most unpleasant experiences suffered by the prisoners. In this study, prisoners would be punished for smiling at a joke, and later punished for not smiling. The effect of arbitrary control on the prisoners was to make them passive and submissive, doing what they were told without initiating any action in case they got into further trouble. In the classroom, arbitrary control may initially be an effective way for the teacher to dominate the classroom and make students listen quietly, but it makes students resentful and hostile and harms their education in the long term.

Real Life Application 1:
Token economies

This article describes Wells Park School in Chigwell, Essex, a residential school for children with emotional or behavioural difficulties (EBD) and one of the foremost training centres for their teachers. Students aged seven to eleven with severe behavioural problems are sent to Wells Park from other schools in Essex and London.

The school's system of behaviour management is based on positive reinforcement and has been steadily refined since it was introduced in 1990. It works because of the consistency and care with which the thirty staff – eight of them teachers – approach their students . Every five weeks, students, families and teachers agree targets of improvement and strategies to achieve them. Children's targets might be 'to use smaller handwriting', or 'to keep still when I am talking to other people' or 'to remember I can be heard using my quiet voice'.

Every fifteen minutes from Monday morning to Friday afternoon, each child has the chance to receive a token. Every day at 3.45 pm after school, the children can cash in their groups of five tokens known as 'giants'. In return they receive treats such as the loan of a tape player, books or toys, an evening activity or extra play. More ambitious spenders can save 'giants' for outings or shopping trips. The tokens allow the teachers to praise and encourage the children. 'It is standard,' [says Principal David Wood], 'for children to increase their reading age by two or three years in the first year they are here.'

Sonia Burnard, head of training at Wells Park, is amused by some of the behaviour programmes that have been used with children in other schools: 'Teachers put a chart on the wall and give the children a gold star now and then. After ten days they say it doesn't work. Nothing will work like that – it's an idiocy. But we have children who couldn't read, who are said to be hyperactive, unteachable really, and we get them sitting down, reading and enjoying life.

'Behaviour management may sound cold,' she says, 'but it's not. It's warm and it's cosy and it's full of love. The tokens aren't really for the children at all. That's the secret. The tokens are for the staff, to remind them to praise the children. That's why it works.'

Adapted from an article by Victoria Neumark entitled 'A token of our appreciation' in the *Times Educational Supplement*, 30 October 1998.

Summary

- Wells Park is a residential school for children with EBD that uses a behavioural management system based on reinforcing 'good' behaviour with tokens that can be cashed in for material rewards.
- The technique used at Wells Park seems very effective, but this may be as much due to the social reinforcement children receive as to the tokens themselves.

Questions

1 The adapted article in RLA 1 claims that behaviour management based on operant conditioning is effective with children who have behavioural and emotional difficulties. Do you think the 'good' behaviour learnt by the children would continue after they leave Wells Park?

2 The evidence in this article is only anecdotal. How would you design a study to demonstrate the effectiveness of the techniques used at Wells Park?

3 The article suggests that the technique works because of the 'consistency . . . of the staff'. Why is consistency so important? What would happen if the staff were not so consistent?

4 Sonia Burnard says that behaviour management of this kind is 'warm . . . cosy [and] full of love'. Do you agree?

Observational learning

In operant conditioning, organisms learn to behave in specific ways by trial and error. This theory ignores certain human mental processes. For example, if a teacher says to a student 'If you don't stop running about I'll send you outside', then the student may modify his/her behaviour without having to try out the alternatives. Similarly, if the members of a class witness a student being punished for throwing pencils around, they may choose to avoid this behaviour in order not to get punished as well. Albert Bandura (1977) recognized the importance of cognitive processes and combined these with operant conditioning theory to come up with the idea that learning occurs mainly through **observation** and **imitation**. By observing others, not only do we learn how to do things, but also we can predict the likely consequences of our actions.

Observation learning starts off with paying **attention** to the **model** in order to learn from them. Clearly this is very important in the classroom: teachers go to great lengths to ensure that their students are paying attention while they are being taught. Second, the behaviour being modelled needs to be *retained* by the observer, as the behaviour is usually required to be imitated at a later time. Bandura suggests **mental rehearsal** (that is, going over the behaviour in your head) is a good way of remembering complicated actions. Finally, the behaviour is performed; this involves reproducing the actions that have been observed and retained, and these actions can be further refined by practice. In order to learn how to do an overhand serve in tennis, a child would observe a model carrying out the serve and make a mental note of the actions involved before trying it out themselves. They would then improve their serve by visualizing modifications to the actions, then carrying them out, not through a process of trial and error but because they have been given advice or have observed other people serving balls.

Bandura describes the ways in which we are motivated to observe and imitate other people's behaviour in terms of reinforcement. For example, it may be that we are **directly reinforced** for imitating others – that is, we receive some kind of reward when we copy someone else. Young children, for example, are taught from an early age that adults, and their

Albert Bandura, who formulated the idea that learning occurs mainly through observation and imitation.

own parents or elder siblings in particular, are suitable role models; toddlers might be praised or encouraged simply because they 'ate up all their dinner, just like Daddy'. If this is true, then children are likely to behave in particular ways simply because they see adults behaving in those ways. Bandura, Ross and Ross (1961) demonstrate this process in their study on aggression. Small children exposed to an aggressive adult model will not only act more aggressively but will imitate the specific actions of the adult. Once a specific behaviour is observed and imitated, it may be that a reward arises as a result; in this case, the behaviour is likely to be repeated, just as it would be according to the theory of operant conditioning.

A second motivation for imitating others is because we see them receiving a reward for the specific behaviour, so we carry it out in order to receive the same reward. This is called **vicarious reinforcement**. By rewarding an individual student for a particular behaviour in front of the whole class, the teacher is encouraging all the other children in the class to imitate that behaviour. Bandura's research of 1965 (see Key Study 2, below) demonstrates this process.

KEY STUDY 2

Researcher: Bandura (1965)

Aim: To show that children will imitate a model to a greater extent if the model is rewarded for his (or her) behaviour than if he is punished or if there are no consequences.

Method: 33 boys and 33 girls from Stanford University Nursery School were individually shown a television programme that depicted a model attacking a Bobo doll for about 5 minutes. (A Bobo doll is an inflatable figure with a heavy base; when knocked over, it swings back into an upright position.) For one-third of the children, the programme ended with the model being rewarded by another adult who came into the room, gave the model sweets and soft drinks, and praised him for being a 'strong champion'. The second group of children saw an ending in which the second adult comes in and shakes his finger at the model, saying: 'Hey there, you big bully. You quit picking on that clown. I won't tolerate it.' He then spanks the model with a rolled-up magazine. The third group saw the model beating up the Bobo doll, but with no consequences at all; no other adult came into the room. Immediately after watching the film, the children were put into another room containing a Bobo doll and observed by two judges through a one-way mirror.

Results: Children in the **model-punished** condition showed significantly less aggressive imitation than children in the **model-rewarded** and the **no consequences** groups. When the children were then offered a reward of fruit juice and colouring books for reproducing the acts of the model, they showed high levels of imitation and there was no difference between the three conditions.

Conclusions: As the children in all three conditions could be induced to imitate the aggressive acts by being offered reinforcers, Bandura concluded that they had all learnt the behaviour by observing the model. However, prior to being offered these inducements, the fact that the children in the model-punished condition showed less imitation supports the notion of vicarious reinforcement – that is, children are more likely to imitate behaviour if they see the model being rewarded and less likely if they see the model being punished.

Observational learning in the classroom
Observational learning in the classroom can occur in a number of ways.

- **Modelling:** the most efficient way to get students to learn how to carry out a complicated procedure is to demonstrate it. For example, a chemistry

A Bobo doll, the 'subject' of a study about imitating behaviours.

teacher will show the class how to carry out a specific experiment before they try it themselves; a maths teacher will sit next to a child and do a sum before setting the child similar examples.

- **Facilitation:** one way of encouraging children to carry out a task that they may be uncertain about is to let them see someone else doing it first. For example, in a swimming lesson some of the students may be too frightened to jump off the diving board. Seeing someone else of their own age doing it may make it easy for them to do it as well, not because they have learnt how to jump off the diving board by observing their classmate, but because they have been given the confidence to try.

- **Inhibition:** children can be discouraged from certain behaviours by observing the negative consequences applied to others. For example, if a child is punished in front of the class, then others may be reluctant to act in the same way. However, the humiliation suffered by the child being publicly punished has to be taken into account before using this technique in the classroom.

- **Disinhibition:** children may be encouraged to act in certain ways because they see others being rewarded for those actions. For example, if a child misbehaves in class and, despite being told off by the teacher s/he gains approval from other children in the class, then others may choose to misbehave in order to gain the same social reward.

Commentary

One of the key features of applying the three behaviourist theories in the classroom is that they all tend to assume that 'teacher knows best'. In operant conditioning, for example, the teacher can manipulate children's behaviour by offering rewards and punishments. It is the teacher who decides what comprises 'good' or 'bad' behaviour, then gets the children to behave in good ways without really discussing it with them first. In observational learning, it is the teacher who decides what a 'good' role model consists of, and chooses to reward certain behaviours publicly in order to encourage other children to copy them. Behaviourists would argue that this is acceptable because the teacher is an adult and really does know best. The relationship between teacher and student is not equal; if a child does not want to sit down and study, then perhaps the teacher has the right, indeed the duty, to get the child to study, for the child's own good.

This is a point of view that **humanist** teachers would disagree with, and we will examine the humanist approach to education in the text that follows.

The humanist approach

Much of psychology is concerned with discovering general laws that govern human behaviour – in other words, in finding out the ways in which human beings are the same as each other. Humanist psychologists, in contrast, are more interested in what makes us individual and unique. Two children in a class, for example, may come from similar backgrounds and have a great deal in common, but if you placed them in the same situation, they might react completely differently from each other. Humanist psychology is based around the idea of a unique '**self**' and, as we shall see, humanists have a very different concept of human nature from behaviourists. This is reflected in very different ideas about education.

Carl Rogers

Carl Rogers (1902–1987) was a key figure in the development of humanist psychology. He was born early in the twentieth century and, as a young man, started training as a scientific agriculturist, then as a theologian, before qualifying as a clinical psychologist. His first job was in Rochester, USA, with the Society for the Prevention of Cruelty to Children, and it is during this period that he began to question some of the traditional Freudian principles of psychotherapy. Freud practised **directive therapy**.

Carl Rogers, a humanist psychologist, developed a number of theories about how learning in the classroom should focus on the student – in other words, a student-centred approach.

Here, the therapist decides what is wrong with the patient and what s/he should do about it, then tells the patient about this decision. However, it began to occur to Rogers that it was his clients themselves who knew best how the therapy should proceed, and this idea later developed into **client-centred therapy**.

A client-centred therapist helps to create a safe environment in which clients can express themselves openly without fear of judgement and can discover for themselves the best way to deal with their own problems. Rogers believed that his clients knew deep down how to solve their own difficulties; all he had to do was help them gain the confidence and **self-esteem** to discover the truth within themselves and take action to improve their own lives.

Rogers saw therapy as a learning process for the client, and he also developed theories about how learning should take place in the classroom. Rogers' concept of human nature and its links to his practice of client-centred therapy are described in the text that follows, as are the implications of his theories for education and what he refers to as **student-centred learning**.

Commentary

Rogers' ideas about education, therapy and the basic nature of human beings were derived from his personal experience as a psychotherapist and not from scientific experiments or controlled observations, and it is for this reason that he has been much criticized by more 'scientific' psychologists.

Scientists argue that in order to show that a theory is 'true', data needs to be gathered from studies that are properly controlled and can be replicated by others. In this way, our conclusions become **objective**, and therefore more valid. If we accept that a theory is true simply because someone says so (that is, truth is **subjective**), then different people may come up with theories that contradict each other, and there would be no proper way of deciding which one was best.

Rogers (1961) agrees with this point of view when it comes to material sciences, such as physics or biology, but points out that in psychology the researcher and the subject of the research are identical (that is, human beings). If you apply scientific methods to the study of human beings, you treat people as if they were material objects and, therefore, you ignore the true nature of human beings. By ignoring people's capacity to surprise us with the decisions they make, you reduce them to the equivalent of programmable robots. Rogers argues that the best way to learn about human nature in general is through insight arising from subjective experience. For example, if you wanted to get to know someone, would you put them through a set of experiments and subject them to a battery of psychometric tests or would you spend a day with them and build up a subjective impression of their nature?

Rogerian theory

Rogers (1951) describes a set of propositions that form the basic assumptions of humanistic psychology. These propositions are summed up in the text that follows on phenomenology, self-actualization, the concept of self and psychological health, and an explanation is given of how they underpin both client-centred therapy and Rogers' notion of student-centred education.

Phenomenology

Phenomenological theory states that individuals see the world in their own unique way and therefore have their own internal reality. This implies that there is no such thing as external reality; the real world consists of what people perceive it to be, and different people may perceive the world very differently. Furthermore, people behave in ways that reflect their own sense of reality.

The therapist needs to empathize with the client and to try to learn as much as possible about his/her sense of reality; an individual's reactions only make sense when seen from the individual's own point of view. However, there is a limit to this process as only clients themselves can be fully aware what their own private worlds are like, so only they can properly make decisions about their own lives.

The teacher must recognize that every child sees the world in a unique way, and that the best way to understand children is to try to see things from their point of view as much as possible. It is important to listen to children and to take seriously what they say.

Self-actualization

Humanist psychologists believe that we are motivated by an innate drive towards self-actualization. At a basic level, this involves survival – getting food to eat, protecting ourselves from threats and so on. We share these basic drives with other animals but, as human beings, we are motivated in a unique way; we want to become 'better people'. Self-actualization means fulfilling our human potential, becoming all that we are capable of being. A self-actualized person is autonomous and free, healthy, competent and creative.

The therapist needs to recognize that each individual, no matter how oppressive his (or her) behaviour, is basically a good person who, if only he were to act out his true nature, would be trying to become even better. There is no such thing as an evil person; we are all born good but some of us are brutalized by our experiences into losing sight of our true nature; this is what makes us do bad things. The aim of the humanist therapist is to help the client move towards self-actualization.

The teacher must recognize that children's true nature is to want to better themselves; the motivation to learn comes from within. Human beings are born with a natural curiosity, a desire to find out about the world around them; the role of the humanist teacher is to facilitate this journey of self-discovery.

The concept of self

We construct a subjective view of what we are like based on our interaction with the world. Our experiences of failure and success, what other people tell us about ourselves, how other people treat us, our beliefs and values all contribute to our concept of self. We then react to our environment in ways that reflect our **self-concept**. For example, a child from a poor background who is mistreated by his/her parents and bullied by other children at school is likely to feel more worthless and incompetent than another child brought up in a privileged culture, surrounded by loving friends and family. As a result,

the second child will behave in very different ways to the first child.

In therapy, it is important for the client to develop an awareness of his/her own self-concept so that s/he and the therapist can understand and interpret the client's behaviour. We all have a self-concept, but are we conscious of what that self-concept is and how it affects our lives? For example, individuals may feel that they are too unlovable to form successful interpersonal relationships, but once they become aware of, and acknowledge, this feeling, they can begin to understand why their relationships tend to fail.

The teacher needs to recognize that some children, due to their upbringing and life experiences, may have a very poor self-concept, and that their behaviour needs to be interpreted with this in mind. For example, a child may become a bully because s/he has developed very low self-esteem as a result of being bullied or abused him/herself. Bullying others is an (inappropriate) way that such children use to feel more worthwhile/powerful/in control. A student may be very bad at meeting work deadlines, not because s/he is idle or unreliable, but because s/he does not feel confident about producing work of an acceptable standard.

Psychological health

According to Rogers (1951), psychological tension is created when there is a discrepancy between the perceived self (what the client thinks s/he is actually like) and the ideal self (what the client would wish to be like). A clear example of this is a person with an eating disorder who believes that s/he is much fatter than s/he wants to be. Psychologically, a person in whom such a discrepancy exists may feel that s/he is not acting like him/herself – that is, not 'being the real me'.

A key aim of humanist therapy is to reduce the discrepancy between the perceived self and the ideal self, to bring the client to accept that 'I am what I am'. One technique is to help clients develop their self-esteem – that is, to raise their perceived self nearer to the level of their ideal self. Another is to help clients reconsider the ideas they have about what an ideal self would consist of. It is vital for the therapist to have what Rogers (1992) refers to as 'unconditional positive regard' for the client – that is, the therapist must value the client as a fellow human being whatever the clients says or does.

The teacher can also help to reduce the discrepancy between the perceived self and the ideal self. In order not to further damage children's self-concept, the humanist teacher must treat his/her students with respect and not, for example, inflict humiliating punishments on them. Humanist education also lays great stress on actually improving children's self-esteem, by providing them with experiences of success, by making the children feel cared for and by giving them positive feedback. The equivalent of unconditional positive regard in the classroom is where the teacher does not withdraw attention or approval from a child who says or does something that the teacher disapproves of.

Commentary

- Humanist psychologists defend Rogerian theory on ethical grounds because, for example, it recognizes that punishment is damaging to the victim and should be avoided for 'human rights' reasons. However, just because Rogers' outlook is positive and optimistic, it does not mean that it is true. It has to be recognized that Rogers has no actual evidence for his theories; they simply consist of assertions that Rogers says are self-evident. This lack of scientific evidence, however, does not mean that Rogers' beliefs are false. In fact, humanists argue that it is not possible to explain human beings using the scientific method without reducing people to the equivalent of machines or animals that do not have self-consciousness. The debate between humanism and behaviourism is not simply an argument about which theory of human nature is more correct, it is also an argument about the methods used to derive such theories.
- The Rogerian concept of self-actualization is sometimes criticized as being too vague and ill-defined. What exactly is a self-actualized person like and would they be recognizable as such by others? Some humanists have pointed to specific individuals as illustrations of self-actualized people (for example, Martin Luther King, Mother Theresa, Eleanor Roosevelt), but these people are not necessarily universally admired by others. If the concept of self-actualization is a relative one, then it becomes less meaningful.

Student-centred education

This section considers in more detail the implications of Rogerian theory for education. These implications will be considered throughout this book, as we look at how humanist teachers would approach specific aspects of teaching – for example, classroom management or dealing with children who have special educational needs. At this stage, the key features of a humanist, student-centred school are that:

- teachers are **learning facilitators**
- **discovery** learning is considered better than **reception** learning
- teachers must be sensitive, caring, genuine, empathetic
- there should be development of **positive self-concepts** in children
- students take part in decisions (classroom democracy versus the 'benevolent dictatorship' of the teacher)
- it is against a performance-orientated, test-dominated approach

In the text that follows we will examine briefly each of these features.

Teachers are learning facilitators
Humanist teachers assume that children have an inner motivation to learn and do not need to be forced to study. This inner motivation expresses itself in a natural curiosity about the world that can be stifled if the teacher imposes a curriculum on students. Children are better off finding out information for themselves rather than being told 'the facts' by a **didactic instructor**.

Discovery learning is better than reception learning
Following on from the last point, the role of a humanist teacher is to present students with questions or problems *that are relevant to them*, provide resources that will allow the students to discover the answers for themselves and help students develop the skills needed to make the most effective use of those resources. Teacher-centred reception learning, on the other hand, tends to consist of the teacher deciding what knowledge the students need to acquire, then presenting it to them for them to learn.

Teachers must be sensitive, caring, genuine, empathetic
Rogers (1961) stresses the importance of the teacher's 'real-ness'; he believed that learning is improved if the teacher expresses his/her true feelings in the classroom and becomes a real person in the relationship with his/her students. This means that it is acceptable for teachers to show their enthusiasm, boredom, anger, insecurity (and so on) in the classroom. However, learning is also improved if the teacher actually feels positive and caring towards students. It is important for the humanist teacher to like children, and to value and respect them. It is also important for the teacher to be prepared to see things from the child's point of view and to empathize with the child. In order to achieve all of

this, the teacher needs to be a caring person, in touch with his or her own feelings and willing to engage in honest interpersonal communication with students.

Development of positive self-concepts in children

Because our behaviour and state of mind is so dependent on our self-concept, it is very important for the humanist teacher to foster positive self-concepts in children. This means enhancing students' self-esteem by, for example, trying to provide them with meaningful experiences of success. Succeeding at a very easy task will not improve a child's self-esteem, but asking students to undertake tasks that are too difficult for them will simply make them feel like failures. Children need to be treated as individuals and have set work at the right level for them. Another way of improving self-esteem is to show students how much they are valued and to give them a sense of empowerment – that is, to make students feel they have some measure of control over their own education. Humanist teachers should avoid anything that actually reduces a student's self-esteem, such as unjustified or negative criticism, public humiliation and so on. Clearly, negative messages can come from other students as well as from teachers, so it is important to help students develop socially and personally, and learn not be unpleasant to each other. The humanist would try to achieve this not, for example, by punishing the playground bully so that s/he does not do it again, but by helping the bully understand why s/he feels so hostile towards other children, and by facilitating general class discussions on the issue of bullying.

Students take part in decisions (classroom democracy versus the 'benevolent dictatorship' of the teacher)

If students are to feel empowered in school, then they need to be involved in all sorts of decisions about what goes on in the classroom. For example, decisions about what to learn (the curriculum), how to learn it, the timetable, how to deal with discipline problems and so on need to be made democratically, involving all the students, rather than imposed by a teacher who feels s/he knows best.

Against performance-orientated, test-dominated approach

Rogers (1961) argues that traditional methods of assessing student achievement are artificial and reductionist; they can only measure certain aspects of education (for example, acquisition of information or specific skills). Other aspects of education,

such as learning to care for other people, gaining insight about yourself, developing positive values and so on are impossible to measure but are, for the humanist, just as important, if not more so.

Commentary

Many of the ideas raised in the text above will be evaluated later in this book (for example, discovery learning versus reception learning; classroom management, assessing student achievement and so on). One evaluation point to be considered here concerns the expectations that humanists make of teachers. They require teachers to be psychologically healthy (for example, in touch with their own feelings), to like children to the extent of being able to provide unconditional positive regard, to be caring, sensitive and empathetic. How many teachers actually satisfy these conditions, and do we have a right to expect them to do so? Can these attitudes be taught as part of teacher training? If so, how? If not, should 'sensitivity', for example, be a requirement of anyone who applies to train as a teacher? If that's the case, how would you decide whether a particular applicant is sensitive enough to become a teacher?

A more practical way of interpreting these conditions is not as a set of criteria needed to be satisfied in order to become a teacher in the first place, but as a description of what humanists would consider to be a good teacher. In other words, rather than expecting applicants to prove that they like children before allowing them on to a teacher training course, we just accept that people who do like children are likely to make better teachers. On the other hand, humanists might argue that teachers should undergo a course of psychotherapy as part of their training, in the same way that therapists do.

Real Life Application 2: Summerhill School

Material A: Extracts from *Summerhill: a radical approach to child rearing* by AS Neill (1960)

In this book, the author describes life at Summerhill, a private school he founded in 1921 and ran according to humanist principles. The school had about fifty students, aged between five and fifteen, including several from overseas. Neill says:

Summerhill began as an experimental school . . . it is now a demonstration school, for it demonstrates that freedom works . . . we set out to make a school in which we should allow children to be themselves. In order to do this, we had to renounce all discipline, all direction, all sugges-

tion, all moral training, all religious instruction . . . All it required was . . . a complete belief in the child as a good, not an evil, being . . . My view is that a child is innately wise and realistic. If left to himself without adult suggestion of any kind, he will develop as far as he is capable of developing.

Lessons are optional at Summerhill; children can go to them or stay away from them – for years if they want to. When children first come to Summerhill from other schools, they exploit their new-found freedom and avoid lessons as much as possible. Left on their own, the children's intrinsic motivation to learn eventually wins through and they attend lessons voluntarily, but the more hatred the child had for his/her previous school, the longer this takes. Neill says:

Perhaps a group of our twelve-year-olds could not compete with a class of equal age in handwriting or spelling or fractions. But in an exam requiring originality, our lot would beat the others hollow . . . In all classes much work is done. If, for some reason, a teacher cannot take his class on the appointed day, there is usually much disappointment for the students . . . A few years ago someone at a General School Meeting (at which all school rules are voted by the entire school, each student and each staff member having one vote) proposed that a certain culprit should be punished by being banished from lessons for a week. The other children protested on the ground that the punishment was too severe.

Staff at Summerhill have a moral objection to examinations but they recognize that some students need qualifications if they want to go on to higher education so the opportunity to take exams is provided, but only if the children want to take them.

Summerhill is possibly the happiest school in the world. We have no truants and seldom a case of homesickness. We very rarely have fights . . . I seldom hear a child cry, because children when free have much less hate to express than children who are downtrodden. Hate breeds hate, and love breeds love . . . Summerhill is a school in which the child knows he is approved of.

Summerhill is run democratically, with staff and students having equal rights; eating the same food, for example, and obeying the same community laws:

At a General School Meeting, the vote of a child of six counts for as much as my vote does . . . But, says the knowing one, in practice of course the voices of the grownups count. Doesn't the

child of six wait to see how you vote before he raises his hand? I wish he sometimes would for too many of my proposals are beaten. Free children are not easily influenced . . . Our children do not fear our staff . . . there is no deference to a teacher as a teacher.

In answer to the question about whether Summerhill is potentially failing children by not encouraging them enough to excel academically, Neill argues that a child's talent in mathematics, for example, is bound to come out if the child is allowed to remain free.

The function of the child is to live his own life – not the life that his anxious parents think he should live, nor a life according to the purpose of the educator who thinks he knows what is best. All this interference and guidance on the part of adults only produces a generation of robots.

Material B: Extract from *The Guardian*, 26 May 1999

The Government will tomorrow threaten to close Summerhill, the independent Suffolk boarding school that achieved worldwide renown for its progressive approach to education, including letting students choose whether to attend lessons and encouraging them to set their own rules.

David Blunkett, the Education and Employment Secretary, intends to file a formal notice of complaint after a damning report by the Office for Standards in Education. He will give the school an ultimatum that it will be forced out of business within six months if it cannot drastically improve student performance, behaviour and standards of education.

The Ofsted report tomorrow will accept that the school has some strengths. 'In general students are well behaved and courteous, if often foul-mouthed. They relate well to the staff and each other,' it says. But the inspectors found serious weaknesses in children's learning. 'The root cause of the defects is non-attendance at lessons . . . some students abandon mathematics for up to two years on end' . . . Students were allowed to mistake 'the pursuit of idleness for the exercise of personal liberty', Ofsted will say.

Zoe Readhead, the headteacher and daughter of the school's founder, AS Neill, said last night the school was bracing itself for a formal notice of complaint.

Summary

- In 1921, AS Neill founded Summerhill, a private school run completely according to humanist principles.
- Children are given a great deal of freedom at Summerhill; lessons are not compulsory, for example. Also, the school is run democratically, with staff and students having equal votes in decisions.
- Recently, Summerhill has come under criticism from Ofsted for poor academic results.

Questions

1 The extract in RLA 2 (Material A) from *Summerhill* illustrates how AS Neill used Rogerian principles as a basis for setting up his school. Which of these principles do you agree with?

2 Students from Summerhill tend to leave with few formal qualifications. Do you think this matters?

3 What kinds of children would benefit from attending a school like Summerhill?

4 Supporters of Summerhill have argued that the problems it faces are caused by the fact that it is only one of very few truly humanist schools in existence and that, if all schools were like Summerhill, then these problems would disappear. Do you agree?

The cognitive approach

Cognitive psychology, the study of mental processes such as **perception**, **memory**, **decision-making** and so on, has some very direct applications to education. Cognitive approaches to education focus on the way in which children learn by acquiring and organizing knowledge. They look at the way in which children's mental skills and abilities change over time, and the impact this has on the strategies they use to learn. Many cognitive psychologists are interested in specific processes such as memory and forgetting; others are interested in broader themes such as the acquisition and use of language.

Cognitive psychologists are interested in both **cognitive** strategies (strategies that relate to methods of thinking that improve or increase learning) and **metacognitive** strategies (strategies that enable students to evaluate their own learning strategies). Metacognition refers to the idea of learning how to learn.

The text that follows focuses on two theorists – Vygotsky and Piaget – whose work is very important in shaping the way we think about cognitive development in the classroom. Both were writing about the cognitive development of children in the early part of the twentieth century, but their ideas have had a lasting impact on the way in which teachers design and implement the curriculum.

Lev Vygotsky

Much of Lev Vygotsky's (1896–1934) work was published in the English language after his death, and was based on research he carried out at the

Summerhill School: *probably the best-known humanist school in existence. But not everyone agrees that the school's approach benefits its students.*

Lev Vygotsky, was interested not only in how children develop on their own, but also how outside assistance can have an impact on this development.

Herzen Pedagogical Institute in Lenigrad in the 1920s and 30s.

Like Piaget (see pages 17–19), Vygotsky was interested in the way in which children become aware of their own thought processes. Children learn many things without really thinking about how or what they are learning – language is a good example of this. It is only as they develop metacognitive strategies that they become able to reflect on their own mental strategies. Metacognitive skills develop considerably later than cognitive abilities. For example, it is relatively easy for a child to learn to speak his/her own language, but as Vygotsky (1962) notes, it is much harder for a child to write at the same level as they can speak. According to Vygotsky, writing is much more abstract; therefore the child has to deliberately think about the sound and the structure of each word, then reproduce it in alphabetical symbols.

For Vygotsky it is this abstract nature of written language that tells us why children's ability to write is less developed than their ability to speak, and not their inability to hold a pencil or form letters. In other words, their metacognitive skills of thinking about, and reflecting on, spoken language is more difficult than simply using it. As Vygotsky argues:

Writing requires deliberate analytical action on the part of the child. In speaking, he [sic] *is hardly conscious of the sounds he pronounces and quite unconscious of the mental operations he performs* (1983, p. 265).

Vygotsky is particularly interested in how social and cultural factors influence the cognitive development of children. Much of his research is based on the transmission of knowledge. By this he means the way in which children learn and use knowledge they pick up from the culture of which they are a part. One of the main ways in which they do this is from other people – for example, their teachers, parents and peers.

One of Vygotsky's most important and influential ideas that leads on from this is that children's levels of development should be measured not only in terms of what they can do on their own, but also in terms of what they can achieve with some assistance. Most standardized tests used at the time Vygotsky was carrying out his research measured the level of development by making children work out problems they would be able to solve alone. Vygotsky argued that this was problematic because it only measured the 'completed' part of the child's development at that time – what Vygotsky called the **zone of actual development**. This zone does not show the true cognitive abilities of the child.

Vygotsky argued that children also have what he called a **zone of proximal development**. He showed this by giving children harder tasks than they could achieve on their own, then giving them a little help – by using a leading question or assisting in the early stages of the problem-solving exercise. He discovered that individual children achieved at quite different levels using this type of co-operative task. Some had larger zones of proximal development than others, and these children, he argued, would do better in school. As he said:

With assistance, every child can do more than he [sic] *can by himself – though only within the limits set by the state of his development'* (1983, p. 268).

A study by Radziszewska and Rogoff (1988; cited in Hetherington and Park, 1999) illustrates a more recent test of this assertion. Radziszewska and Rogoff asked a group of nine-year-olds to plan a shopping trip around a town. In one condition the group of nine-year-olds were paired with children of their own age, and in the other condition a different group were paired with one of their parents. The pairs had to plan the trip in order to buy certain things and also to make the most economical journey (by not retracing their route, for example, and by visiting certain shops and not others).

The results of the study showed that the children planning with the parent made better and more efficient plans than the children planning with another child. Children with an adult often planned out the whole route before they started and studied the whole map to do so. Children paired together did not plan like this and found it more difficult to work co-operatively. Children who had worked with an adult were also able to use what they had learned and plan similar tasks in the future more effectively than the children who had worked with their peers. As Vygotsky suggested, children benefited from the assistance of an adult and the transmission of knowledge in this particular way.

Commentary

The implication of these points for classroom practice is that, first, Vygotsky suggests the teacher is very important in the process of the transmission of knowledge. This means the teacher must take great care that the knowledge he/she imparts is accurate and useful to the child. Secondly, Vygotsky suggests that children need teaching that stretches them, and that this is at a higher level than their own development. If children are not taught in this way they cannot use their zone of proximal development and therefore are not able to reach their true potential.

Jean Piaget

Jean Piaget (1896–1980) started his academic life as a biologist, and his later understanding of cognitive development was greatly influenced by this early work. He saw cognitive development as a way of organizing and adapting to the external environment, in much the same way as any biological organism adapts to its environment. At the age of 21 he had finished a PhD in biology and turned his attention to psychology, an area in which he had developed a growing interest over the previous few years. After a couple of years in Paris he had the opportunity to work with Binet, who was one of the first people to use standardized tests on children and is widely credited with being one of the first people to develop intelligence testing. Working with Binet, Piaget became interested in the mistakes children made in these tests, and thus the research for which he became so famous was started. Piaget was a prolific author, and his theories about the cognitive development of children generated an incred-

ible amount of research and debate throughout the twentieth century.

Piaget's research techniques were quite controversial when he started his research. At a time when most of psychology concerned itself with rigorous control and hypothesis testing, Piaget developed a technique that became known as **clinical-descriptive** (Wadsworth, 1996). Piaget's work was mostly observational, although it was very systematic. He asked children questions, then analyzed their answers in detail. Piaget carried out research on many aspects of cognitive development in children. A full analysis of his work would take volumes; the text that follows discusses the four basic concepts Piaget uses to explain how cognitive development occurs:

- schemata
- assimilation
- accommodation, and
- equilibration.

Schemata

Schemata (schema, singular) can be defined as categories that the individual uses to organize the world. Piaget describes the mind as having structures in much the same way as the body does, and these structures (schemata) adapt and change as the child grows and develops. A young child will have fewer schemata than an older child or adult. The younger child cannot organize his/her world in terms of very complex categories – everything has to be dealt with and categorized in simple ways. Schemata reflect the child's current level of understanding and knowledge of the world. Piaget argues that these schemata are 'constructed' by the child, and therefore they are not true reflections of reality; this is something that develops with time (**constructivism** – the idea that knowledge is constructed by the individual – was a radical view to Piaget's contemporaries, many of whom were behaviourists who subscribed to learning theories). As children grows their ability to differentiate between objects and experiences grows with them, and they learn to make more sense of the world and all that happens by categorizing these experiences in more complicated and sophisticated ways. The processes that allow change and development to occur within these schemata are **assimilation** and **accommodation**.

Jean Piaget, whose theories about the cognitive development of children generated much research and debate throughout the twentieth century.

Assimilation

This is the cognitive process by which people are able to integrate new information into existing schemata. The schemata do not change, but they may grow to take in new information. Assimilation is a continuous process, and Piaget argues that people can assimilate a great deal of information at any one time. As children get older they learn to assimilate increasing amounts of information. Assimilation is part of the process enabling people to adapt cognitively to the world around them. However, assimilation can only help us to understand a growing amount of knowledge. Piaget argues that for the categorization of knowledge to change, a different process has to take place. He states that actual changes in schemata occur through the process of accommodation.

Accommodation

This describes the way in which schemata have to adapt when faced with information that cannot easily be assimilated. For example, if a child with relatively few schemata with which to explain the world is faced with information that does not fit in to existing schemata, s/he has to accommodate the information in some way. In order to do this the child can either create a new schema to accommodate the information, or s/he can change or revise an existing schema to do the same thing. Piaget describes both of these as forms of accommodation. Once the child has made this accommodation s/he can then assimilate the new information. Assimilation is always the outcome of accommodation.

Accommodation accounts for development (a qualitative change) and assimilation accounts for growth (a quantitative change); together these processes account for intellectual adaptation and the development of intellectual structures (Wadsworth, 1996, p. 19).

Equilibration

Equilibration is the process that regulates assimilation and accommodation. These two processes must be balanced if the child is to develop cognitively in a 'normal' way. Not being able to assimilate information causes **disequilibrium**. This is put right by the process of accommodation through which the child regains equilibrium. Piaget believed that disequilibrium (as a state of imbalance) is a motivating force for children to either assimilate or accommodate new information. Equilibrium is therefore a state of cognitive balance, and equilibration is the term Piaget used to describe the process by which this occurs.

It is through the process of assimilation and accommodation that the environment is organized and structured. Schemata are the products of this organization.

Piaget looked at the way in which children develop cognitively, and how their ability to assimilate and accommodate new information might affect the learning process. Some of the work for which Piaget is most famous concerns the developmental stages of children. Piaget identified four main stages through which children pass in their cognitive development, and he argued that these stages influence what they are ready to learn; if they are not ready then children will not be able to learn with understanding.

Piaget argued that the mistakes children make in any stage show what stage of cognitive development they have reached. He recognized that children of the same age might vary in their cognitive ability, according to their intelligence and social environment (Piaget, 1969), but he argued that children have to pass through the same series of stages in their cognitive development.

Piaget's work has had very far-reaching implications for educational practice and policy. The curriculum has to be designed with children's cognitive ability in mind. For example the curriculum should:

- provide physical and mental activity
- provide optimal difficulty – to enable children to both assimilate and accommodate new information
- understand the limitations of children's thought processes and be able to assess their readiness to learn new ideas
- provide opportunities for children to engage in social interaction with their peers and teachers.

It is no use trying to teach children ideas and concepts they are not ready to learn, and this also has implications for 'success' and 'failure'. There are obvious consequences of children finding that they cannot do what is asked of them – and they can easily learn to dislike topics they cannot grasp. As Kegan argues:

People grow best where they continuously experience an ingenious blend of support and challenge . . . Environments which are weighted too heavily in the direction of challenge [cognitive demands too high] without adequate support are toxic . . . Those weighted too heavily in the direction of support without adequate challenge [cogni-

tive demands too low] are ultimately boring . . . (1994; cited in Wadsworth, 1996, p. 42).

Commentary

The work of Piaget and Vygotsky is often compared. Piaget is the better known of the two, because although they were contemporaries, Vygotsky died young. Piaget was a very prolific author and became widely known and respected. Their ideas are similar in a number of ways and differ in others.

- Both Piaget and Vygotsky are constructivists that is, is they both see knowledge as a construction. They disagree on the way in which the knowledge is constructed (see the next point).
- Piaget has often been accused of ignoring the importance of social and cultural factors affecting the development of knowledge, whereas Vygotsky was particularly interested in this. Piaget believed that children construct their own knowledge, based on assimilation and accommodation, whereas Vygotsky believed that children construct knowledge that is transmitted more directly from those with whom they interact. Piaget saw the role of the teacher as one in which they should stimulate and support the student, whereas for Vygotsky the teacher acted as a model for the child.
- Piaget believed that the cognitive stage of development the child had reached limited how much they could learn, whereas Vygotsky was interested in how the zone of proximal development could be achieved with support.
- Piaget did not look at individual differences or at individual variation in the construction of knowledge.

Metacognitive strategies

This section on the cognitive approach has focused on the work of two very important theorists, and we have not looked in any detail at particular metacognitive strategies that students might use to enhance their learning. In the introduction to this chapter we listed some of the specific processes (such as memory and forgetting) that cognitive psychologists are interested in. Memory, for example, involves the use of cognitive strategies such as **rehearsal** (repeating what the person is reading or hearing) and **organization** (grouping or arranging information together). A metacognitive strategy in relation to memory would involve the student in developing particular techniques to enhance their own ability to remember and recall information. In other words, metacognitive strategies involve

the process of thinking about the best ways of learning.

Real Life Application 3:
Key Skills in Curriculum 2000

The application outlined here involves the development and use of metacognitive strategies in the curriculum as part of a deliberate attempt by the government to recognize the achievement of students' skills as well as their knowledge.

Key Skills have been a part of the curriculum for some time and have been a familiar part of GNVQ qualifications, for example, for a number of years. Recently, however, attention has turned to the need to introduce Key Skills into the GCSE and A level curriculum. The rationale for this is to develop and accredit the skills that students need to acquire in order to study and learn effectively. A Key Skills qualification can help students to develop learning strategies within an educational framework, and gives them evidence of skills that will be useful in the workplace.

The Key Skills qualifications that are currently being devised develop skills in:

- communication
- application of number
- information technology
- working with others
- improving own learning and performance
- problem-solving.

There are many ways in which working with the Key Skills specifications develop and use the learning strategies of a student, including gathering, organizing and remembering information. Using the Key Skills specifications also requires that students evaluate their own performance, which is an important metacognitive strategy in working out learning strategies that suit them best.

A Key Skills qualification in the curriculum recognizes also that students do not always learn in the same way at the same level. There are different levels that can be awarded for the attainment of differing levels of expertise. Level 3 is the one that is recognized to be at A level standard; however, a student can develop a profile of Key Skills that is at different levels for some of the skills.

How the Key Skills qualification is taught in your own school or college will depend on the way in which your programme of study is organized; so this will vary from college to college, although the qualification remains the same. Some institutions will advocate an integrated approach to Key Skills in which much of the Key Skills teaching and accrediting will go on within the programme of study. Others will plan a separate course for Key Skills that runs alongside the main area of study, and some will develop a mixture.

Summary

- As part of the Curriculum 2000 initiative, the government has recently introduced a Key Skill qualification, aimed at providing students with cognitive strategies for learning.
- There are 6 Key Skills areas, and qualifications can be achieved in these at 4 different levels.
- Some schools or colleges will teach and assess Key Skills as part of other examined courses, whereas others will provide stand-alone courses in Key Skills.

Questions

1 How do you think Key Skills should be taught in your own school or college?

2 Is it educationally useful to teach Key Skills to post-16 students?

3 Do you think that it is useful to provide students with the opportunity to gain a Key Skills qualification?

Example essay questions

1 Describe the ways in which different general psychological perspectives have been applied to education.

2 Describe and contrast the ways in which behaviourist and humanist psychologists gather evidence to support their theories.

3 Describe and compare the basic assumptions about human nature made by behaviourist, humanist and cognitive psychologists.

4 Compare and contrast a classroom run along behaviourist lines with one run according to humanist principles.

2 Teaching and learning

The aim of this chapter is to show how behaviourist, humanist and cognitive approaches are linked to the ways teachers teach and assess learning. The first section examines assumptions about children's motivation to learn and how this can be improved. In the second section, the work of Gagné, Bruner and Ausubel, and the implications of their ideas for teaching and learning, are described. The chapter ends with a discussion of the purpose and effectiveness of different forms of educational assessment. Real Life Applications that are considered are:

- RLA 4: Predicting exam grades
- RLA 5: The power of feedback.

Motivation consists of the forces or pressures, whether internal or external, that make us behave in certain ways. In education, students need to feel motivated in order to achieve success in their studies.

Motivating students

Some children are very highly motivated; they enjoy studying and are keen to do well and, as a result, are more likely to put a lot of effort into their work and to attempt difficult tasks. Other children do not enjoy learning, are much less confident of their ability to succeed, are much more afraid of failing and so are less likely to attempt work that may be challenging. What is it that makes some children more highly motivated than others, and how can teachers motivate their students? The strategies a particular teacher employs are linked to his/her view of what motivates human beings in general.

In developing theories of motivation, psychologists are trying to discover what it is that initiates, encourages or prevents human behaviour. This source of behaviour could come from within the person or from the environment.

Theories of motivation

The text that follows looks at several historical theories of motivation, then goes on to examine behaviourist, humanist and cognitive theories in more detail.

Instinct theory
Non-human animals can behave in very complex ways without ever being taught how to. Stickle-backs, for example, have a sophisticated mating ritual that they carry out even if they are separated from other sticklebacks at birth (Tinbergen, 1952). Clearly, these fish must be born with the motivation to carry out this behaviour somehow pre-programmed into their brains. Complex, inherited behaviour such as this is called an **instinct**. In 1859, Charles Darwin published his famous work entitled *The Origin of Species by Means of Natural Selection*, and it became clear that humans are much more like other animals than people had previously thought. It seems reasonable to assume that human behaviour is also motivated by instinctual urges, at least in part. Freud believed that motivation was largely instinctual and described several human instincts: **libido** (the sex drive), **ego** (the self-preservation instinct) and **thanatos** (the aggressive, destructive instinct).

Drive theory
Drive, or **need**, theory is based on the assumption that tensions, or **dissonance**, are created in an organism when there is a disequilibrium between the internal and external environment. These tensions are uncomfortable and the organism seeks to relieve them by appropriate action. For example, lack of food leads to hunger, which drives the organism to seek food.

Drives necessary for bodily survival are called **primary** (for example, hunger, thirst, sexual behaviour), while **secondary** drives are acquired (for example, money). Unlike instinct theory, drive theory does not assume the existence of complicated innate blueprints for behaviour. Instead, it suggests that organisms, including humans, have evolved specific drives to help them survive.

Commentary

Instinct and drive theories assume that human beings are subject to internal urges that they cannot control. However, humanist psychologists would argue that a key difference between humans and other animals is self-awareness and self-determination, and that this enables us to overcome our urges by applying 'higher' influences such as notions of justice or fairness. Also, humans are much more affected by social factors than other animals. It may be that we have instincts and drives built into us, but their influence is negligible compared to social, cultural and psychological influences.

Psychological hedonism

At first glance, the theory of psychological hedonism seems simple and obvious: it states that we act in ways that maximize the pleasure we receive and minimize the pain. If we enjoy the outcome of a certain behaviour, then we will do it again. For example, children are motivated to learn because they enjoy it, and if they do not enjoy it, then they will not do it. However, this theory does not explain *why* we enjoy certain activities. For example, one child may derive enjoyment from running around the classroom and another from sitting at a desk doing some arithmetic. So if a child does not enjoy studying, how can s/he be motivated? Despite this problem, the idea that we act in certain ways because of the pleasure it gives us was taken up by behaviourists and developed into their theories of reinforcement.

Arousal theory

Arousal can be psychological (alertness, attentiveness, wakefulness) or physiological (increased pulse, breathing rate and so on). The Yerkes-Dodson Law states that the level of arousal is related to motivation in a particular way (see Figure 2, next column). If a student is under-aroused, for example, then s/he will feel apathetic or bored and will not perform well. On the other hand, over-arousal leads to stress and anxiety, and this can lead to loss of motivation. This means that there is an **optimal** level of arousal at which the individual is at his or her peak of motivation and performance.

Another assumption linked to this theory is that individuals strive to maintain the optimal level of arousal. So, for example, if a child is bored in class, then s/he will attempt to increase arousal, maybe by talking to a friend or walking around the room. If a

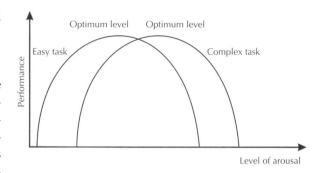

Figure 2: The Yerkes-Dodson Law of Arousal

student is stressed by the demands of a particular teacher, then s/he may reduce arousal by missing the next lesson in order to avoid the teacher.

Commentary

If teachers assume that their students are not working hard enough, they could try to increase their arousal levels by increasing the demands in class or pointing out how important and difficult the forthcoming exams are, for example. However, teachers need to be careful that they do not encourage high levels of anxiety, because their students will not work well if they are too stressed. In practice, this can be a difficult balance to get right. It is also important for the teacher to ensure that students do not become bored and under-stimulated in lessons, nor made anxious by work that is too demanding or difficult. Again, this is difficult to achieve.

Behaviourist versus humanist approach to motivation

The theory of psychological hedonism (see previous column) suggests that people behave in ways that give them pleasure and avoid pain. Behaviourists are not interested in the concepts of pleasure and pain, because these are internal feelings, and therefore not susceptible to objective observation and measurement. Instead, behaviourists simply define the concept of reinforcement as an outcome that increases the probability of particular behaviours occurring. For example, if experience shows that praising a child for working hard makes it more likely that s/he will work hard in future, then we know that children can be motivated by praise, and any thoughts or emotions the child may experience are irrelevant.

In order for reinforcement to be effective in motivating children, it is important to follow these principles.

- The learner must be aware of exactly what behaviour s/he is being rewarded for.

- The reward must be given as soon after the behaviour is performed as possible.
- Rewards must be offered in a consistent manner.
- The teacher should start off by giving frequent rewards (continuous reinforcement), then gradually reduce them (partial reinforcement).
- The teacher must not be over-generous in offering rewards; this can actually lower motivation.
- The teacher should make sure that every child in the class is able to earn a reward at some time.

The behaviourist notion that behaviour can be modified or controlled by manipulating the external or extrinsic rewards offered to a child has been criticized by some psychologists as mechanistic and dehumanizing. Humanist psychologists, in particular, stress the importance of internal or intrinsic rewards. An intrinsic reward can be described as a good feeling from within that results from a specific behaviour. For example, if a student completes an essay on time and is praised by the teacher, s/he is receiving extrinsic reinforcement. On the other hand, if the student feels a sense of achievement and satisfaction at having completed his/her work, then this constitutes intrinsic reinforcement.

If humanists are to argue that individuals are motivated by intrinsic reinforcement, then they need to explain where this intrinsic reinforcement comes from, or at least what it consists of. Abraham Maslow (1908–1970), an important humanist psychologist, takes a pragmatic approach to this problem. He does not attempt to answer the question about where human motivation comes from; he simply describes what he thinks human beings are motivated by. He developed a **hierarchy of needs** based on his experience as a psychotherapist and psychologist; these needs form a hierarchy because they start off with the basic survival needs that humans share with other animals, then move up towards more sophisticated needs that are unique to human beings (see Figure 3, below).

Maslow referred to the first four levels of needs as **deficiency needs** because, if these needs are not satisfied in an individual, then s/he is physically or psychologically deficient – that is, unable to survive and live more or less happily. The next three levels of needs are **growth needs**, and it is these that motivate us to learn and study. Maslow argues that the lower level needs must be satisfied before the person can concentrate on higher level needs. For example, it is very hard to persuade a student to learn about poetry in class if s/he is not getting enough to eat or feels physically threatened every time s/he goes home. However, once the more basic needs are satisfied, then motivation comes from within. This is the philosophy of Summerhill School (see RLA 2, page 13) where children are free to choose whether to go to lessons or not. Teachers at Summerhill do not consider it necessary to provide incentives (or punishments) in order to encourage children to attend classes; they argue that when given complete freedom to choose what to do, children will want to attend lessons because of their intrinsic need for knowledge and understanding.

Abraham Maslow, a psychotherapist and psychologist who devised a 'hierarchy of needs' for all human beings.

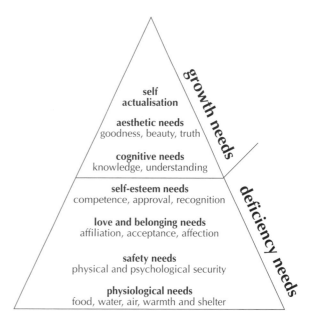

Figure 3: Maslow's hierarchy of needs

Commentary

At first glance, it may seem that behaviourist and humanist theories of motivation do not conflict with each other; behaviourists simply observe which specific rewards lead to an individual repeating a behaviour, and humanists describe the needs that these rewards are satisfying. However, Maslow's hierarchy of needs contains elements that cannot come from outside the person. It is possible to say 'well done' to a child and therefore satisfy his or her self-esteem need for recognition, but the satisfaction of having successfully solved a maths problem comes from within. In fact, all of Maslow's higher level growth needs are intrinsic in nature and cannot be satisfied by a teacher. Humanists argue that the growth needs are the ones that motivate children in education whereas behaviourists would deny the very existence of internal growth needs.

Furthermore, humanists would argue that, attempting to motivate children to learn by giving them extrinsic motivation undermines their intrinsic motivation. If a child is doing some work in order to get a gold star, for example, s/he might become over-dependent on the approval of the teacher and lose sight of the intrinsic benefits of doing the work. The study by Lepper and Green (1975) clearly illustrates this process (see Key Study 3, below).

KEY STUDY 3

Researchers:	Lepper and Greene (1975)
Aim:	To measure the effects on children's motivation of extrinsic reinforcement and surveillance by adults.
Method:	80 four- and five-year-olds from a nursery school located on Stanford University campus were taken individually into a room containing a table holding a set of puzzles, a television camera and a set of attractive toys hidden by a cloth screen. One group of children were shown the toys and told they could play with them if they worked hard on the puzzles (extrinsic reinforcement); the other group were not shown the toys. In both conditions, the experimenter left the room and returned after the child had completed six puzzles. All the children were told they had done a good job with the puzzles and were allowed to play with the toys for ten minutes, but it was made clear to the first group that this was reward for having done so well on the puzzles. The second group were offered the toys in a **non-contingent** manner – that is, the reward was not linked to a specific behaviour; they were told that the toys happened to be there and that they could play with them if they wanted to. Two weeks later, the puzzles were set out in the children's classrooms alongside other activities that would normally be there. The children were observed by two people, from behind a one-way mirror.
Results:	Significantly fewer of the children who had been offered the toys as a reward for doing the puzzles chose to play with the puzzles two weeks later (70 per cent versus 92 per cent).
Conclusions:	The children who expected a reward for doing the puzzles were less likely to play with them when no reward was offered. On the other hand, the children who were not initially offered a reward to do the puzzles may have derived satisfaction and enjoyment from them, and were more likely to choose to do them again. It seems, for this study, that offering children extrinsic reinforcement for an activity can actually undermine the intrinsic satisfaction they derive from that activity.

Cognitive theories of motivation

Cognitive psychologists argue that people make conscious decisions to behave in certain ways rather than simply responding to external reinforcement (the behaviourist approach) or to internal needs (the humanist approach). For example, a student does not write an essay just in order to receive praise from the teacher or out of an inner thirst for knowledge, but as a result of a rational assessment of the likely outcome of writing the essay; in other words, the student *decides* to write it. Cognitive psychologists attempt to describe how and why we decide to do things; part of this is to explore the links between the decision-making process and our **attitudes** – that is, our opinions and our values. The text that follows looks at how two types of attitude – **attribution** and **self-efficacy** – are linked to motivation.

	Internal	**External**
Unstable	Effort	Luck
Stable	Ability	Difficulty

Figure 4: Ways in which people attribute their successes and failures

Attribution

People make attributions (that is, find explanations for behaviour) in several different ways. First, attributions can be **internal** or **dispositional** (that is, due to the individual's personality or intentions) or **external** or **situational** (that is, due to the situation an individual is in, the environment, other people or even chance). For example, consider the following interaction between a student who is late for a lesson and the teacher.

Student: 'It's not my fault I'm late; I slept in.'
Teacher: 'Well, you should've set your alarm clock earlier.'
Student: 'I did, but it's not loud enough to wake me.'
Teacher: 'You should get a louder alarm clock then' and so on . . .

The student is making an external attribution in order to avoid getting into trouble, whereas the teacher is trying to persuade the student to make an internal attribution in the hope that if the student accepts responsibility for being late, s/he might do something about it in future.

Second, attributions can be **unstable** (that is, temporary) or **stable** (that is, permanent). If as student does well in a test, for example, a stable internal attribution would be 'I am clever', whereas a stable external attribution would be 'These tests are always easy'. An unstable internal attribution might be 'I revised really hard for this test', whereas an unstable external attribution would be 'I did well because I was lucky'.

Third, attributions can be **global** or **specific**. If a student fails a maths test, then an internal stable global attribution would be 'I failed because I am hopeless at everything, including maths'. It is not difficult to see how someone making this kind of attribution may feel de-motivated. Figure 4 (see next column) shows the interaction between internal/external attributions and stable/unstable attributions.

Psychologists have shown that people make errors in the way they attribute behaviour. There are certain types of attribution errors that we all have a tendency to make. Nisbett *et al.* (1973), for example, describe the **actor–observer effect**, in which we have a tendency to attribute our own behaviour externally and other people's behaviour internally (which is what is happening in the dialogue between the late student and the teacher above).

Apart from these general attribution errors, each of us has a specific **attributional style** – in other words, we have a tendency to attribute behaviour in certain ways and to make specific types of attributional errors. For example, over-confident people tend to attribute success to internal, stable and global reasons ('I did well in my biology test because I am brilliant at everything'), and they attribute failure in an external unstable and specific way ('I failed my biology test because it contained questions that we had not been told to revise').

This raises two important questions for the teacher. First, in what ways does an individual's attributional style affect his or her motivation? Second, how can we change the way students make attributions in order to improve their motivation?

We can answer the first question by looking at some examples. Students who attribute failure at academic tasks to internal stable causes (that is, lack of ability or aptitude) are less likely to persevere with their work than students who attribute failure to internal unstable causes (that is, lack of effort). The student who attributes his/her lateness for lessons externally (for example, 'It wasn't my fault if I slept in') will be less likely to do something about the problem than the student who accepts responsibility for being late. The child who attributes success internally ('I succeeded because I am good at it, or I tried hard') is more likely to attempt similar tasks in future, especially if they attributed their success globally ('I could succeed at anything if I try hard enough'). On the other hand, the child who feels that his/her success is due to external causes ('I was lucky') may feel less motivated in the future. Clearly, then, attributional style is linked to the extent to which people *persevere* with their learning, and also with the degree to which they are prepared to take *risks* in the future.

Most attempts to change students' attributions in order to improve motivation have aimed to shift perceived **locus of control** from external to internal, so that children feel they are more in control of the outcomes of their own behaviour. In other words, they take responsibility for their own learning and, as a result, put more effort into their studies. Teachers can try to do this by talking to students and trying to convince them that they are responsible for what happens to them, but it is important that students' actual experiences in school reinforces this. For example, work set by the teacher has to be of a level such that a student can succeed if s/he puts the effort in (repeated failure may make a child feel that s/he could not succeed even if s/he tried really hard), but not so easy as to make the student feel that anyone could have succeeded. Students must not be placed in situations in which they can blame their success or failure on chance.

Finally, students need to be taught specific skills that will enable them to succeed; these metacognitive strategies (see RLA 3, page 19) will make students realize they can do something specific to help themselves become more effective learners, and this will increase their sense of personal control and their motivation.

Self-efficacy

Attribution theory shows how the ways in which we account for our past successes and failures can affect how we rate our chances of success in future. Our perception of our own competence or ability to succeed is referred to as **self-efficacy**. This evaluation of our own personal effectiveness forms part of what Carl Rogers referred to as the perceived self (see Chapter 1, pages 10–13) and the value we put on our perceived self comprises our self-esteem. Clearly, high levels of self-efficacy are likely to be linked to greater motivation; children who feel more confident that they can succeed are more likely to undertake tasks and will show greater perseverance at them. In order to understand how teachers can foster a greater sense of self-efficacy in students, it is necessary to explore the factors that contribute to high or low levels of self efficacy. Bandura (1986) describes four different influences that can affect self-efficacy.

1 **Enactive influences:** this refers to the individual's past experiences of success and failure. Someone who is used to being successful will feel more confident about succeeding in future (unless, of course, s/he attributes his/her success largely to external factors; see page 25). It is therefore important for teachers to provide their students with **experiences of success**, by making sure the tasks they are set are easy enough for the student to stand a good chance of success, but not so easy that the student feels no sense of achievement.

2 **Vicarious influences:** this consists of comparing oneself with others and judging our own competence accordingly. This means that teachers should be careful about reading out marks in class or creating academic competition in the classroom, as this could make some students feel less competent. One of the major criticisms expressed when Standardized Assessment Tasks (SATs) were first introduced into primary schools was that for every child who performs above average there is another who performs below average. This second child's sense of self-efficacy will suffer if public comparisons in test results are made (see the text on assessing educational performance, pages 33–37).

3 **Persuasory influences:** Bandura suggests that an individual's self-efficacy can be enhanced by other people persuading him/her to undertake the task in question. If a student is reluctant to tell a story in front of other children through lack of confidence, say, the teacher could make him/her feel more able to carry out this task successfully by providing reassurance and encouragement.

4 **Emotive influences:** Bandura suggests that over-anxiety may lead an individual to feel that s/he is not capable of succeeding at a specific task. As explained in the section on 'Arousal theory' (see page 22), teachers need to make sure that students are aroused enough to feel motivated, but not so aroused that they feel that they cannot manage.

The self-fulfilling prophecy

It is often said that teacher expectations of students is a key factor in their motivation and achievement. If teachers have high expectations – that is, if they believe that their students will do well – then somehow this makes it more likely that their students will indeed do well. This process is called the **self-fulfilling prophecy**; teachers form impressions of students and develop expectations of how well they expect them to perform (note that these impressions could be tainted by prejudice relating to ethnicity or gender, for example; see text on cultural differences, pages 56–64). The teacher's behaviour is bound to be affected by his or her attitude towards a student, and the student is bound to pick up on the teacher's expectations of him/her, even if this all happens at an unconscious level. The student then behaves according to the teacher's expectations. In this way, teachers can motivate children by having high expectations of them (but not too high, or else the student will fail to meet the expectations and may lose their sense of self-efficacy). Conversely, they may demotivate students by not expecting enough of them.

Rosenthal and Jacobson (1968) carried out a study that demonstrates the self-fulfilling prophecy in a dramatic way. It must be noted that this study is controversial; some psychologists have since failed to replicate its results, while others claim they have confirmed Rosenthal and Jacobson's conclusions.

Key Study 4:

Researchers: Rosenthal and Jacobson (1968)

Aim: To demonstrate that teacher expectation can influence children's achievement.

Method: The study was carried out in Oak School, an elementary (that is, primary) school in a working class area of San Francisco. The school consisted of six year groups, each split into three streamed classes. The teachers were initially told that the purpose of the study was to validate a new psychometric test designed to predict **academic blooming** (that is, the extent to which children would improve intellectually). The test was entitled the 'Test of Inflected Acquisition', and teachers were told that it would be sent back to Harvard University for scoring and for the data to be processed. In fact, the children were given a standard intelligence test. Five children were chosen at random from each class, and the teachers were told informally that these children had scored highly in the test and were therefore really going to improve academically during the coming

year. Over the next year, the children were given the same intelligence test three more times. The teachers were also asked to describe the classroom behaviour of all their students.

Results:
1 The intelligence test scores of the children who had been named as potential 'bloomers' improved significantly more than those of the other children.
2 The self-fulfilling prophecy effect was stronger for the younger children.
3 The children who had been designated as 'bloomers' were rated by teachers as more curious, more interesting and happier than the other children.
4 Out of the children who had *not* been designated as bloomers, those who showed a greater improvement in IQ were actually rated *less* favourably by the teachers.
5 The children who received the worst ratings from teachers were those in the lower sets who had not been designated as 'bloomers' but who had improved *most*.

Conclusions: Rosenthal and Jacobson concluded that teacher expectation does have an effect on student achievement. They also said that children who break teacher expectations, even if they do better than expected, are seen by teachers as less well-adjusted, particularly if they are from a below-average ability set.

Real Life Application 4:
Predicting exam grades

Predicting exam grades is a way in which teachers formally set out their expectations of students. They do this for several reasons.

- To provide information for prospective colleges, universities or employers.

- To pass on to exam boards in case students are prevented from sitting examinations as a result of illness and so on.
- To let students and/or their parents know how well they are getting on with their studies.
- To motivate students.

Whatever the reason for predicting grades, it is clearly important that they are accurate. For example, if a student's predictions are too low, then s/he may not get the offer from a university that s/he deserves, or may become discouraged. On the other hand, some students may be motivated to work harder by receiving low predictions. If the predictions are too high, then students will receive university offers that they cannot fulfil, or else they may become over-confident about their progress in a particular subject.

How accurate are predicted grades? There is little research in this area. Statistics produced by some exam boards seem to suggest a fairly close match between predicted and actual grades (with predictions, on average, one grade higher than actual results), but they tend to compare the total number of grade Bs, say, predicted by a school with the total number of grade Bs achieved by the students. This does not necessarily mean that the every student who was predicted a grade B actually got one. Research in a particular sixth form college a few years ago suggested that teachers were accurate in about 50 per cent of cases. The reason that teachers get predicted grades wrong may simply be that predicting grades before exams are taken is actually very difficult for any student. The solution to this is to create systems that do not rely so heavily on predicted grades. For example, there has been much talk of sixth form students applying to University *after* they have received their A level results. Alternatively, it may be that teachers are making systematic errors in predicting grades. It would be interesting to see whether there are any patterns in the mistakes teachers make when predicting grades in relation to gender, ethnicity or class.

The self-fulfilling prophecy theory would say that predicting low grades can actually contribute to under-achievement and vice versa. In other words, if a teacher thinks that a students is not going to do very well in a certain subject, and predicts a low grade, the student may do less well than if the predicted grade had been higher. This may happen as a result of two factors.

1 The student may become discouraged and de-motivated as direct result of being told that s/he is expected to do badly.
2 The teacher may react differently to students who are expected to get low grades.

On the other hand, predicting high grades may actually help students achieve more.

As a result of the difficulty of predicting exam grades accurately, and the potentially harmful consequences of getting it wrong, some teachers are uncomfortable about having to produce predictions, even if they see it as a necessary part of their job.

Summary

- Predicted grades serve a variety of purposes and are produced by teachers at various stages in a student's career.
- Teachers often get predicted grades wrong, and it is possible that this actually affects student achievement.

Questions

1 From your own school experience, how accurate have your teachers been in predicting your grades?

2 Do you think that teachers' predictions of your grades have had any influence on your performance or achievement?

3 Describe initiatives that could be introduced with the aim of completely removing the necessity for teachers to predict grades.

Teaching methods

The text that follows considers some of the theories discussed in Chapter 1, and looks at how these can be applied to teaching and learning methods. Obviously, a teacher may use a behaviourist or a humanist approach in their teaching style. For example, a teacher who used behaviourist strategies might use particular forms of operant conditioning in their classroom such as some kind of token system (see pages 4–6). They may be more didactic in their approach, preferring their students to sit still and listen. A humanist, on the other hand, may prefer a more open approach, encouraging the students to explore ideas for themselves.

Regardless of the underlying theoretical perspectives, most teachers share certain practices in common; and in reality, of course, they will use a mixture of techniques depending on the situation and the type of lesson they are teaching. However, some obviously favour certain methods over others. Before looking at the actual methods of teaching and learning, it is important to look at the goals that underpin these methods.

It is important that students understand the purpose of their lessons so that the material they learn has meaning – both within the individual lesson and within a whole syllabus or scheme of work – particularly for older students who are focusing on exams. If they cannot see the purpose of their lessons or do not understand the content, students are likely to lose interest and motivation. For this reason lesson planning has to be undertaken with care. Teachers structure the work that students do in lessons for perhaps a term or even a whole year, so there are always particular goals and objectives.

Teachers' lesson plans often use terms such as 'student goals' or 'learning outcomes', as it is very important to be sure what students will gain from a particular lesson. Tyler (1974; cited in Borich and Tombari, 1997) argues that as society becomes more complex so there is more to learn. However, he also acknowledges that there is less and less time in which to teach this information. This means that teachers have to make choices and focus on what is really necessary. Although Tyler was writing almost 30 years ago his ideas apply to contemporary education systems perhaps more than ever before; teachers feel increasing pressure with initiatives such as the National Curriculum, Literacy and Numeracy hours each day in all state primary schools, and the changes that Curriculum 2000 will make.

Changes in government legislation about the delivery of the curriculum, particularly the introduction of the National Curriculum, have affected both the teaching and the learning strategies that are used in the classroom. The full effects of Curriculum 2000 have yet to be felt, but it is obvious that there will be major changes in the organization of teaching and learning. The increase in the number of AS exams or GNVQ modules, alongside Key Skills qualifications, for example, is going to increase contact time between students and teachers, and will involve careful planning in order to ensure that students understand the relevance of all their areas of study.

Tyler argues that teachers should develop the goals of their teaching based on five factors:

1 The content of the curriculum
2 Knowledge that is valued by society
3 The interests of the student
4 The educational philosophy of the school
5 Theory on educational teaching and practice.

These factors include an interesting mix of practical considerations and wider concerns, which again can be seen to have contemporary relevance in the way in which they reflect current concerns. It could be argued that knowledge that is currently valued by society includes the kinds of skills that will be covered in the new Key Skills qualification.

Tyler discusses the goals with which teachers should be concerned. However, goals do not actually explain the types of method or style a teacher or learner might use. Therefore, the text that follows looks at the work of theorists whose ideas have had a significant impact on the way in which teachers actually deliver the curriculum.

Robert Gagné

Robert Gagné (1916–) is a cognitive psychologist who is interested in what are called learning outcomes. He looks at these as the end product of the students' learning and argues that the teacher must first identify the desired learning outcomes in order to plan the way in which students will achieve them. In other words the teacher must decide what the student needs to learn and the best way to teach it. Gagné (1985) describes what he considers to be the five types of learning outcomes:

Robert Gagné's ideas are particularly important because of his focus on the effect that teaching methods have on students.

- verbal learning
- intellectual skills
- cognitive strategies
- motor skills
- attitudes.

Each of these is looked at in more detail in the text that follows.

Verbal learning

Verbal learning refers to the ability to name objects, places and understand the meaning of words. It is one of the first stages in the process of learning, as without it a child cannot continue to develop the intellectual skills listed below. Theorists such as Gagné refer to the order in which children learn as a **learning hierarchy**. It is important to understand that children have to learn things in a certain order, as they need to assimilate new information on the basis of information they have previously acquired.

Intellectual skills

Gagné describes different types of intellectual skill that children need to learn. For example, **discrimination learning** involves the child being able to understand the difference between things, the differences between colours, letters of the alphabet or numbers. Discrimination learning is a stepping stone to **concept learning**, which is a second intellectual skill that Gagné identifies. Concept learning involves children being able to understand that objects can be grouped together – for example, types of trees or cars. Gagné also differentiates between concepts and defined concepts. Defined concepts are more abstract and can only be understood with reference to other concepts – for example, concepts such as prejudice or happiness.

The most difficult intellectual skills a student will learn are rules. Gagné argues that rule learning is difficult because it is one thing to know a rule, but quite a different thing to apply it. Children often know the rules of grammar, but do not apply them to their own writing or speech, for example.

Cognitive strategies

Gagné describes the need for students to be taught to use cognitive strategies in order to learn (these types of strategy were outlined in Chapter 1; see pages 15–19). For example, particular strategies have to be developed for learning how to spell a word or to add up two numbers, as well as learning for a test or solving a particular problem.

Motor skills

Motor skills refer to accurate movements that children develop. Alongside the other skills a child learns, Gagné highlights the need to learn motor skills in a classroom setting. The most obvious example is learning to write clearly, and teachers spend a lot of time enabling children to practise this motor skill. PE lessons also teach students motor skills, and they may practice these in and outside of lesson time.

Attitudes

Gagné takes a behaviourist view of the way in which school can influence the development of attitudes. He recognizes that attitudes are affected by reinforcement and argues that teachers should be aware of the need to encourage students so that their experience of school is a good one. Positive reinforcement is therefore important all the way through a student's school career. Additionally, Gagné argues that students' attitudes are also likely to be affected indirectly through imitation – of their teachers and peers, for example. So, again, he notes the importance of fostering good relationships within the school environment, as teachers are obviously very powerful role models – especially early on in a child's schooling.

The implication of Gagné's approach to the classification of learning outcomes is that a teacher must plan his/her delivery of the curriculum very carefully, so that teacher and student both understand the nature and purpose of the learning strategy. Perhaps more important than the work of individual teachers in this respect is the need to plan the whole curriculum and the order in which it is taught. In common with many other cognitive psychologists, Gagné is interested in the hierarchy of learning (see previous column). For example, a child cannot learn how to group numbers or shapes in sequences or patterns (concept learning) before s/he has learned the names of all the objects s/he is grouping (verbal learning).

There are many other classification schemes for defining learning outcomes, most of them the work of cognitive psychologists. They are similar, but each has a slightly different focus. Another well-known classification of learning outcomes comes from the work of Bloom *et al* (1956).

Commentary

- Gagné's ideas have much in common with the work of other cognitive psychologists who focus on the need to build knowledge in a structured way. All cognitive psychologists argue that individual students will construct their own knowledge based on what they have already learnt.

- The first point leads into the second; that the cognitive approach is different from the behaviourist one. The behaviourist approach would suggest that all students experience and learn the same things, while cognitivists would argue that each student will experience the teaching and learning process in different ways.
- One of the criticisms of Gagné's approach is that his classification of learning outcomes is too broad and does not include the behaviours of students that show whether they have learnt a particular strategy. Some of the other classification schemes are more specific and include a description of these behaviours – for example, Bloom *et al* (1956).

Jerome Bruner, a psychologist whose theories are associated with what is known as 'discovery learning'.

Different approaches to teaching and learning methods
The work of two other theorists – Jerome Bruner and David Ausubel – will be covered in the text that follows. Bruner and Ausubel are also cognitive psychologists, but their work illustrates two very different approaches to teaching and learning methods. Bruner's theories are associated with what is known as **discovery learning**, and Ausubel's theories are associated with what is known as **expository teaching** or **receptive learning**. Although both these psychologists work from a cognitive perspective it could be argued that humanist approaches to teaching and learning underpin the ideas of Bruner, while Ausubel might be recognized as more behaviourist in his approach to teaching styles.

The text that follows also examines two other related learning styles – **cognitive apprenticeships** and **co-operative learning**.

Jerome Bruner

Bruner's (1915–) ideas have a lot in common with those of Piaget. Piaget states that we learn through interacting with the environment, and that through this interaction we assimilate and accommodate new information. By doing this learners construct their own knowledge. Bruner (1961) states that learning is an information-processing activity, by which students try to understand their environment. According to Bruner, students do this by organizing and categorizing information using what he calls a coding system. He believes that the most effective way to develop a coding system is to discover it rather than being told it by the teacher –

hence the term 'discovery learning', which he uses to describe this learning method. (The approach is also referred to as a constructivist approach; this refers to the fact that students construct the knowledge for themselves; see Chapter 1, pages 17–19).

A good teacher will help students to discover the relationships between facts by themselves. This means that the teacher has to design lessons so that students are able to discover for themselves the relationships between different bits of information. To do this the teacher must give students access to the information they need, but without organizing it for them. The students themselves will then organize and sort the information, learning in the process what the teacher wants them to know. Bruner believes that when students are presented with material that is too highly structured they become too dependent on others whereas if they are allowed to discover things for themselves, they will remember the information longer and be able to apply it to 'real life' situations.

The role of the teacher is what Bruner refers to as a mediator. The teacher must not direct the student too much, but needs to give enough guidance to enable the student to have the means to learn.

One of the terms that Bruner (1961) uses to describe the way in which information should be taught is the **spiral curriculum**, to enhance discovery learning. The use of a spiral curriculum involves repeatedly presenting ideas over a period of time – in a simple form at first, then in more complex ways as the student gets older and is able to understand more sophisticated concepts.

David Ausubel

David Ausubel, is associated with what has become known as 'expository teaching' or 'receptive learning'.

Expository teaching (sometimes referred to as **direct explanation teaching**) is the name given to the type of approach that Ausubel (1918–) believes is the most effective. What is interesting about this approach is that although it is often presented as completely teacher-led, Ausubel (1960) actually argues that it is constructivist because the student is not a passive recipient of information, but actively learns from it. The outcome of expository teaching is reception learning. The student receives the information from the teacher, rather than discovering it for themselves.

Ausubel (1977) discusses what he calls meaningful learning; not all reception learning is meaningful. For learning to be meaningful Ausubel argues that the teacher must explain how new knowledge can be integrated into existing knowledge; relationships between pieces of knowledge and prior learning must be made explicit. Ausubel argues that most teaching and learning in the classroom is expository and receptive, not least because discovery learning is very time consuming by comparison. Ausubel also argues that there is no conclusive evidence to suggest that discovery learning is better than reception learning.

Ausubel suggests presenting material in certain ways to make it meaningful. One example is to use what he calls **advance organizers**. This is a term used to describe the way in which the teacher should start the lesson by presenting concepts to the students to focus their attention on the relationship between the lesson content and prior learning. Ausubel describes two different types of advance organizers: expository and comparative. An **expository organizer** is a descriptor of relevant concepts

(in other words, the concepts are being exposed to the learner). A **comparative organizer** is a presentation of how the knowledge about to be learned compares to, and fits in with, existing knowledge.

Whether or not teachers advocate the use of discovery or reception learning, it is very likely that they will use Ausubel's advance organizers. It is good practice to remind students what they covered in previous lessons and to explain how what they are about to do builds on what they have already learnt.

Commentary

- These two approaches to teaching and learning are not mutually exclusive. As was suggested at the beginning of the chapter, teachers are likely to use both methods as they find them appropriate in relation to what they are teaching.

- Although these two views are often presented as 'opposing' views, there are in fact many points of comparison rather than contrast. Both are cognitive approaches, and both therefore place an emphasis on the understanding of new material in terms of what the learner already knows and their organization of knowledge. Both believe that the learner is an active 'information processor'.

- As cognitive approaches the ideas of Bruner and Ausubel are both constructivist and contrast with more objective ideas about knowledge, which suggest that knowledge exists outside and independent of the individual.

- However, while both Bruner and Ausubel are cognitive psychologists, Bruner's ideas are more closely linked to the work of Piaget, and appear to be a humanist approach to teaching and learning. In contrast, Ausubel's approach appears to be more closely linked to a behaviourist view of teaching and learning.

- It is difficult to determine the superiority of either approach, as both have their merits. As has been discussed, Ausubel argues that there is no proof that discovery learning is more effective than reception learning. Ausubel also argues that children cannot discover very much that is meaningful to them without considerable direction from the teacher. Interestingly, however, Ausubel does recognize that discovery learning has a place for younger primary school age children, but argues that after the age of eleven or twelve years, it becomes a waste of time.

- One of the most important factors that will influence the effectiveness of the two approaches is the personality of the teacher and his/her own individual teaching style. Some expository teachers might be inspirational to their students, while others might make the information they are imparting unintelligible.

- A teacher may prefer an expository style, but students might still discover new relationships for themselves and organize the material in a way that is meaningful for them as individuals.

Co-operative learning

Co-operative learning is a humanist approach that relates most closely to the idea of discovery learning. Rather than working as individuals competing against each other, students are put into small groups to work together – and the success of the group depends on all the members working together for a common goal.

Slavin (1991) argues that this type of approach encourages interpersonal skills and positive self-esteem. He also argues that this type of approach promotes higher levels of academic achievement than more individualistic approaches.

Commentary

One of the problems with co-operative learning is that although it is thought to raise self-esteem and enhance communication skills, it relies on each member of the group making a significant contribution. If one member of the group does not co-operate effectively, there might be an unfair burden of work on the other members. Moreover, the student who is less involved will gain little from this type of activity.

Assessment of co-operative learning has to be individual, so that each member of the group is assessed on the basis of their own participation. Work should be written up and handed in separately for marking to ensure not only that each student has done their share but that they all understand the task that was set.

Cognitive apprenticeships

The idea of cognitive apprenticeships is that students need to learn skills as well as knowledge. Importantly, students need to learn for themselves how to gather and use information that they need. Having knowledge is no use unless it can be used in a meaningful way. This is something that is sometimes neglected in the classroom; teachers are so concerned about covering the curriculum (often using expository techniques) that they have little time left to focus on the skills that students will need in order to use the information – for example, in an exam. Those who advocate an approach focused on cognitive apprenticeships argue that the student is a

novice who will be apprenticed to learn from the teacher (expert).

Models of cognitive apprenticeship share common features, such as teaching cognitive and metacognitive strategies, and focus on specific curriculum areas such as reading, numeracy and writing. They all describe the expert teaching skills that enable a novice to learn strategies that are specific to a particular area (Borich and Tombari, 1997). Other strategies involved in cognitive apprenticeships are the use of modelling, coaching, scaffolding, articulation and reflection (Borich and Tombari, 1997).

- **Modelling** involves the teacher explaining the idea, and showing the novice how to understand and apply it to his/her own context, so the student can imitate the teacher.
- **Coaching** is the guidance and support a teacher offers a student while s/he attempts to imitate the teacher.
- **Scaffolding** is the support a teacher offers while the student practices – it is important that there is not too much scaffolding or too little, so the student has adequate support, but the teacher is not solving the problem for the student.
- **Articulation** involves the learner explaining what s/he is doing – to the rest of the class for example, so that the teacher can make sure the student understands what s/he is learning.
- **Reflection** involves the learner comparing his/her own approach to that of the teacher, and reflecting on his/her particular strategy.

This approach offers both the expository teaching of the expert and the discovery of the beginner, and appears to combine the ideas of both Bruner and Ausubel.

Assessing educational performance

The text that follows looks at the various types of assessment that are used within the education system. Teaching and learning relies on assessment, not always to judge performance but also to understand how students learn and to diagnose what they need. It is almost impossible not to assess, and there are many ways in which teachers try to assess progress. These range from observing to standardized testing.

There are now many more forms of assessment than there used to be. In the 1960s, for example, there were very few formal assessment procedures in place. There was the eleven-plus exam, which was used in what is now Year 6. This IQ test was used to determine which kind of secondary school a child should progress to (see Chapter 4, page 62). There were also O and A levels, which were usually taken at age sixteen and eighteen respectively. Then there were university exams for about 7 per cent of all 21 year olds. In the year 2000 there are now SATs for seven, eleven and fourteen year olds. There are GCSEs at age sixteen, and AS and A2 exams at age seventeen and eighteen. There are also GNVQ assessments and Key Skills qualifications. At degree level, 35 per cent of all 21 year olds will take final examinations (Child, 1997). The emphasis is now obviously on standardized testing to assess students' performance, and it is seen as necessary information for teachers, students and parents, as well as being used for government league tables.

One of the most important issues is how to make assessment constructive and as objective as possible. Assessment is often seen as competitive and results in success or failure, rather than being a record of a person's strengths and developments. Teachers need assessment, but they have to be able to use both their own judgement and standardized tests to measure their students' progress and understanding.

Within this framework teachers have to be very sensitive about stereotyping their students, both with the use of formal and informal assessment. A great deal depends on the way in which the assessment is used and the response of the individual students to the task; students can often become anxious when they are being tested, which will obviously distort the nature of the assessment. Children learn the meaning of assessment at quite an early age and this can have implications for the type of assessment that should be used. For example, after the age of eight, children become aware of the difference between trying to do something and actually achieving it; and they become aware of competition, when they see the difference between their own performance and that of others. The problems of this awareness are that some children who find it easy to do well might stop making the effort and, in particular, those who see themselves 'failing' in relation to their peers might stop trying altogether.

Children do expect their work to be assessed by their teachers, but this can have both positive and negative consequences as it can motivate them to work well or it can make them worry too much about the assessment and not enough about the actual task. The same can also be said of teachers, who sometimes have to focus on the exam the students will take at the expense of broadening the curriculum.

Some material is easy to test. Factual information, for example, can be tested with short-answer questions, whereas the skills of evaluation and understanding are harder to assess. Materials that do test these almost inevitably limit the opportunities for students to show their ability. For example, a short-answer maths test may be relatively easy to assess, using ticks or crosses, whereas marking an essay may be seen as much more difficult and subjective. There is an important distinction to be drawn here, because a teacher would not fully understand his or her students' abilities unless s/he also looked at their conceptual understanding and their ability to show a whole range of skills. Few forms of assessment are used in isolation.

Types of assessment

There are four main types of assessment tool:

- formative
- diagnostic
- summative, and
- evaluative assessment.

Formative assessment
This gives an indication of the stage that a student is at, in order that a teacher can plan the curriculum effectively. Formative assessment can be carried out before a task or stage has begun (sometimes referred to as **pre-task** assessment), or used once a course of work is underway to check progress and development, and to give feedback to students. Examples of formative assessment include observation, discussion and the use of measurement tools such as IQ tests. Essay marking and giving feedback is also an example of formative assessment.

Diagnostic assessment
This is used to discover any problems that a student might have – for example, a specific learning difficulty. For the most part this is carried out alongside formative assessment, within this stage of a child's educational career (although obviously problems sometimes get overlooked or misdiagnosed). A cognitive ability assessment such as the British Ability Scale (BAS) may be used in the first instance, then individual tests for the problem that is suspected.

Summative assessment
This is concerned with judging the overall achievement of a student and to measure the outcomes of

learning. For example, SATs and GCSEs and A level exams are summative. These are not only used to judge overall achievement, but are also sometimes used to predict future performance.

Evaluative assessment

This is concerned with evaluating the whole performance of a class or school, often in relation to other classes or schools in order to check their performance against others. Examples of evaluative assessments are inspection reports and government league tables based on exam performance at, for example, A level or using SATs results.

The first two types of assessment are to help with the child and his/her particular development; they are widely used by teachers and educational psychologists in schools all the time. The last two are concerned with checking that the child is being taught and supported in appropriate ways; they are used less frequently to judge how well students, teachers and schools are doing. It is important to understand the way in which students learn, and assessment obviously helps with this. However, assessment can also be used to highlight the differences between schools and students, and this can have negative implications as well as positive ones.

Although we have used the term evaluative assessment to describe the way in which schools and colleges are assessed externally, it is important to distinguish between *assessment* and *evaluation*. Slatterly (1989) states that assessment shows the nature and extent of a child's learning, and evaluation is what comes after assessment. Evaluation involves judgements about the effectiveness and worth of what the assessment has measured. For example, a child may be assessed, then a value given to the level of the assessment. A student may be assessed, then a school may be evaluated on the basis of its students' performance in the assessment tasks.

Assessment does not always have to be formal, as suggested earlier; it might involve something as potentially subjective as observation. Testing, for example, is only one form of assessment, and is by its very nature a limited one. Assessment that is fair involves a wide range of evidence being taken into account.

Commentary

Because there are so many ways of assessing students there are a number of different evaluation points that can be made of different types of assessment.

- Some forms of formative and/or diagnostic assessment are ethnocentric and favour certain groups in the population. As mentioned, many of the tests are now written in a culturally specific way and address the needs of different groups of students (for a discussion of the problems with IQ testing, see Chapter 4, pages 70–71).
- Diagnostic testing can be very helpful to the teacher and the student, but there are sometimes problems with the way in which a teacher may subsequently stereotype the student (and also with the way the student may stereotype themselves).
- The results of diagnostic tests are sometimes difficult to interpret and often need a specialist (educational psychologist) to administer them.
- Summative tests, such as short-answer questions or a knowledge-based exam, can be straightforward, easy to administer and mark, but are quite limited in the type of information they can test.
- Summative tests – for example, exams – can also be quite artificial. They may be reliable but lack validity, and therefore may not be a true representation of a student's capabilities (for a discussion of reliability and validity, see pages 36–37).
- Summative assessment that uses essay-type questions can test skills and understanding, but can be difficult to mark.
- All assessment can have negative implications, as has already been discussed, and there are many ethical considerations; not only the stress that assessment may cause the student, teacher or school, but also the ethics of using assessment in the first place. Certain types of assessment may be deemed unnecessary, or unfair (some types of evaluative assessment may fall into this category) at least for those who are subjected to them.

Criterion and norm-referenced assessment

Students can be assessed in relation to other students or they can be assessed against set standards. These two ways of measuring are known as **criterion** and **norm-referenced** assessment.

- **Criterion referenced assessment**: this is assessment based on a set standard against which students' work is measured. The criteria for achievement are set out in a mark scheme, for example, for a piece of coursework or an exam.
- **Norm-referenced assessment**: this is assessment that compares students with each other. This means that students might be ranked according to their performance or, in the case of diagnostic

tests, for example, their performance might be measured against a norm for children of their age or ability.

These two types of referencing are useful for different types of assessment. Formative assessment may be both criterion referenced and norm referenced. Diagnostic assessment is likely to be norm referenced. For example, the British Ability Scale, used to measure cognitive ability in a number of ways, was norm referenced on 3,000 children when it was first designed and is checked every two years with a group of 1,500 children. Summative assessment is assumed to be criterion referenced, but it is also norm referenced because if everyone got A grades or first class degrees then it would be assumed that standards were going down, not up. For example, as students improve their A level grades year on year, there are reports in the media about A levels getting easier.

Reliability and validity in assessment

There are different forms of reliability and validity, and some of them are relevant to assessment. It is very important that assessment is both reliable and valid if it is to be effective and useful. One of the major concerns that students have is whether assessment (in whatever form) is fair.

Reliability

If a method of assessment is reliable then it must be consistent in the way it measures whatever it sets out to measure. A simple example of a test that should be reliable is an IQ test, as the score would be expected to remain constant (give or take a few points). An exam or test could be said to be reliable if it gives a consistent result from one occasion to the next, regardless of who marks it. If the test scores fluctuate then either the exam questions or the person marking them is unreliable.

There are several forms of reliability that are useful in the context of the need for consistent assessment.

- **Test-retest reliability** was described previously. If a student took the same test twice s/he should get the same result if the test has test-retest reliability (excluding the possibility of a practice effect).
- **Split-half reliability** looks for internal consistency within the measurement tool. If the test is divided in half, and both halves are measuring the same thing, then the scores on the two halves should be similar. For example, the different sections on an exam paper, or the two halves of a spelling test, should have split-half reliability.
- **Alternate forms reliability**, as its name suggests, looks for reliability within two different forms of the same test. For example, an IQ test or a diagnostic test for dyslexia should give a similar score for the same student, whichever version s/he takes.
- **Inter-rater reliability** means that if two different people mark the same exam, for example, they should come up with the same result. This is clearly an important requirement for any test, but it is not always easy to achieve, especially in subjects in which the mark scheme is open to interpretation. Teachers and exam boards spend a great deal of time engaged in a process called **moderation**, in which different examiners mark the same papers and compare results in order to achieve maximum consistency. Despite these efforts, there is often a **tolerance** of several percentage points between different examiners.

Validity

Any form of assessment can be reliable but not valid. It could measure something consistently but not be measuring what it as intended to measure. The meaning of validity in the context of assessment is that the test measures what it intends to, and if it does not do this then it is of no use. As with reliability, there are several types of validity. Those that are relevant to assessment include the following:

- **Face validity** – which means that a test looks as though it measures what it intends to. This type of validity is perhaps more important for the student, who needs to be reassured by looking at a test that it is appropriate.
- **Content validity** – which is very important in educational terms. A test that does not measure the knowledge and/or skills that relate directly to the content of the course the student has been studying cannot be very useful. A test has to be constructed and analyzed very carefully to ensure that it covers the range of material and skills a student ought to have achieved.
- **Predictive validity** – which is the validity the test has as a measure of the student's future performance. If they have predictive validity, A level exams and SATs tests, for example, should be accurate predictors of how well the student will perform in the future. The expectation that this is

true is reflected in university offers to students on the basis of their predicted grades.

- **Concurrent validity** – which is the validity that comes from two different assessment tools giving the same measurement of performance. These can be correlated to see if the diagnostic tests, for example, give the same cognitive ability ratings or memory scores.

Real Life Application 5:
The power of feedback

In an article published in the *Times Educational Supplement*, Maureen O'Connor looks at the effects of formative assessment and argues that overall standards rise if assessment is used to identify students learning needs. She cites research carried out by researchers at King's College in London that looked at 600 research studies from all over the world, and involved more than 10,000 learners. The studies show that assessment that diagnoses students' difficulties and that provides specific and constructive feedback, leads to an improvement in learning. These studies were carried out at all levels of the curriculum and across a range of very different subjects.

The differences in learning were estimated using experimental groups and comparing their learning with groups of students taught in the normal way. O'Connor describes an example of a Portuguese study of 246 children with 25 teachers. These children were given learning objectives and assessment criteria by their teachers, then asked to rate their own performance on a daily basis. The study showed that children in the experimental group progressed twice as fast as those in the control group.

The researchers at King's College conclude that it is the quality of the feedback given by teachers that is one of the most crucial factors if formative assessment is to be a success. Their survey indicates that there are five factors that are crucial for success, and five that are detrimental.

Factors crucial for success include:

- regular classroom testing (to improve learning and teaching – not for competitive use)
- clear, meaningful feedback
- the active involvement of all the students
- careful attention to the levels of self-esteem and motivation of each student

- self-assessment by the students (both in groups and with the teacher).

Factors limiting success include:

- tests that are superficial and encourage learning by rote
- failure of teachers to review testing procedures with each other
- over-emphasis on marks and grades at the expense of meaningful advice
- too much emphasis on competition between students (instead of focusing on personal improvement)
- feedback, testing and record-keeping, which is for managerial purposes rather than learning purposes.

The problem that researchers identify in Britain is that although formative assessment is recognized as important the education system is geared towards summative assessment (SAT tests, GCSEs and A levels, for example).

O'Connor ends her article with the observation that perhaps the reduction in the content of the curriculum due to start in September 2000, will allow teachers to focus on formative assessment more fully.

(NB: the introduction of a Key Skills qualification may also have this effect.)

Article adapted from *Times Educational Supplement*, 6 February 1998.

Summary

- There is evidence that assessment that diagnoses students' difficulties and that provides specific and constructive feedback leads to an improvement in learning.
- However, the British education system is geared towards summative, rather than formative, assessment.

Questions

1 What kinds of formative assessment have your teachers used with you during your school career?

2 Which of these have you found most effective and why? Try to think of some reasons not listed in the article.

Sample essay questions

1 Explain and evaluate ways of motivating using extrinsic reinforcement.

2 Describe and evaluate the different teaching methods that might be recommended by a cognitive psychologist.

3 Discuss the differences between diagnostic and formative assessment, and evaluate the ways in which they might be used in the classroom.

3 Managing the classroom

This chapter is about managing the classroom, both in terms of dealing with behavioural problems and with the physical classroom environment. It describes the different types of behavioural problems that may be encountered in a classroom and the variety of techniques for dealing with them. Real Life Applications that are considered are:

- RLA 6: Social inclusion: pupil support
- RLA 7: Wonder drug or playground curse?
- RLA 8: Fostering pro-social behaviour
- RLA 9: How to be a good teacher
- RLA 10: The soft classroom.

Problem behaviour in the classroom is generally defined as behaviour that is dangerous, offensive or disruptive, and many teachers describe dealing with such behaviour as the most difficult and stressful aspect of their work. Problem behaviour lies along a spectrum ranging from mild, everyday 'naughtiness' to extremely dangerous or disruptive behaviour.

Behavioural problems

Children who frequently display such extreme behaviour and who persistently fail to respond to corrective strategies employed by teachers are labelled as having emotional or behavioural difficulties (EBD). Such children are often excluded from mainstream schools and may be temporarily sent to local behavioural support units or for more long-term treatment to special EBD schools. An analysis of official statistics for the 1997/98 academic year reveals that 12,300 students were excluded from school (including 1,500 from primary schools) and that around two-thirds of those students never returned to mainstream education (research published on 14 February 2000 by Include, a charity campaigning for the reintegration of excluded children).

Recent education policy in the UK has moved away from excluding such children and towards trying to help them within mainstream schools. A circular issued to schools by the Department for Education and Employment (1999) entitled 'Social inclusions: pupil support' lists several ways in which schools can deal with EBD students. These include:

- setting good habits early – primary schools need

to set high standards of attendance, punctuality and behaviour from the start
- early intervention – dealing with problem behaviour as soon as it occurs
- rewarding achievements – for example, certificates or prizes for good behaviour/attendance
- involving other students – for example, in anti-bullying and harassment policies, and through Schools Councils
- identifying underlying causes – for example, providing additional literacy/numeracy support if necessary
- providing study support – for example, homework clubs and thinking skills workshops.

Commentary

- The debate between exclusion or segregation (that is, educating children outside mainstream schools) and inclusion or integration will be examined in more detail in Chapter 4 (see pages 68–69). Meanwhile, two criticisms can be made of the proposals in 'Social inclusion: pupil support' described earlier. First, they take time to implement and, although they may benefit teachers in the long term, it is difficult to see where teachers would get this extra time from. Second, they seem to ignore underlying emotional difficulties; although dealing with these would be well beyond the resources or expertise of most schools at present, it could be argued that any attempt to cope with EBD children that does not tackle their emotional problems is doomed to failure.
- Although there often is a consensus among teachers,

parents and educational psychologist about 'diagnosing' a particular child as EBD, this is not always the case. The difficulty is that there is no objective definition of 'problem behaviour'. In practice, the forms of behaviour that are labelled as problematic are those that are unacceptable to the particular teacher or the school. Such behaviour can vary a great deal from school to school, and even between different teachers in the same school. The specific behaviours considered unacceptable by an individual teacher will depend on his/her teaching style and general approach to education, so that humanist teachers may accept, and even welcome, behaviours from students that behaviourist teachers are not prepared to tolerate. Also, teachers may find specific behaviours unacceptable because of their own personalities, attitudes and experiences. For example, some teachers become particularly upset when their students skip lessons; this could be because this makes them feel insecure, inadequate or rejected, or maybe they feel that it is a challenge to their authority, or perhaps because it makes them feel more anxious about their students achieving good exam results. Such teachers are likely to be much stricter about attendance.

- Does it matter if different schools, or even different teachers in the same school, have different standards of classroom behaviour? Some teachers argue that this is confusing to children and that staff trying to impose a stricter regime are undermined by more lenient colleagues. On the other hand, perhaps children are capable of adapting to different standards in different classes and it is wrong to try to impose classroom management rules onto individual teachers. In practice, most schools have general rules, enforced by all teachers, but there is also a variety of practice in individual classes.

The text that follows focuses on four specific types of behaviour: conduct disorder, bullying, attention deficit hyperactivity disorder (ADHD) and school refusal. These are forms of behaviour that would be considered problematic by all teachers and that often lead to children being excluded from school.

Conduct disorder

This is sometimes referred to as **delinquency** and consists of behaviour that is especially anti-social – such as lying, stealing, vandalism and violence. Many children act in these ways from time to time, but children with conduct disorders do so persistently, and this can make them very difficult to manage in the classroom. There is a range of possible causes for conduct disorder, including adolescent rebellion, genetic/biological causes, poor 'discipline' at home, and economic and social deprivation. Each of these causes is covered in more detail below.

Adolescent rebellion
There is evidence that the physical changes that occur during adolescence can make young people's moods particularly labile (that is, changeable). Also, many adolescents feel that society, and parents in particular, treat them like children when they feel they belong to the grown-up world. Furthermore, adolescence is a time when people try out different patterns of behaviour and experiment with attitudes and personalities before establishing a more stable adult identity. It is important to treat adolescents with respect and understanding, so that they can develop a strong sense of identity and of social responsibility.

Genetic/biological causes
A disproportionate number of children excluded from schools for conduct disorder have special educational needs, and these are often linked to genetic factors or birth complications (for example, cerebral palsy, dyslexia, hearing impairment and poor memory). Furthermore, some medical conditions – for instance, asthma, epilepsy and allergies – have been linked to conduct disorder. It is also possible that conduct disorder is linked to hereditary personality traits, but research in this area has been inconclusive so far.

Poor discipline at home
Children of parents who are extremely lax are more likely to show conduct disorder, but then so are children of over-strict parents, or parents who use physical punishment or show a lack of affection or attention. Perhaps the most damaging discipline is when it is inconsistent (see Chapter 1, pages 5–6).

Economic and social deprivation
There is a strong correlation between child delinquency and poverty. However, the reasons for this are not clear. For example, children of single mothers are more likely to be convicted for crimes: is this because these children have no fathers to provide moral guidance, or rather because single parent families tend to be less well off? Are working class children more likely to display conduct disorders because of a clash between the school ethos, which is likely to represent more middle class values, and the home environment? Or does being poor simply make it harder to be a good student?

Commentary

Chapter 2 (see pages 25–26) described how people attribute behaviour internally or externally, and this issue is very relevant here. If a child displays emotional and behavioural difficulties in the classroom, whose fault is it? There is a tendency to blame individual children for their anti-social behaviour in the classroom, but there is a great deal of evidence to suggest that teacher behaviour is an important factor in generating or preventing conduct disorder. Mortimore *et al* (1988; cited in Riding and Rayner, 1998) identify several aspects of school management that are effective in reducing conduct disorder. These include:

- consistency among teachers
- structured, well-planned lessons
- intellectually challenging teaching
- a work-centred focus within lessons
- maximum dialogue between teachers and students
- good record keeping (personal/social/academic)
- a positive climate.

It could be argued that a school that does provide the right conditions for learning is actually responsible for encouraging good behaviour in its students.

Bullying

School bullying can take many different forms and is very prevalent in our schools. A significant proportion of students are involved in bullying, either as victims or perpetrators, and the effects of bullying can be serious. Victims of bullying suffer a loss of self-esteem, which can have an adverse effect on their lives in many different ways, or they can simply be put off school and education in general. Bullies themselves, apart from running the risk of getting into trouble at school, are significantly more likely to become involved with the criminal justice system later in life.

Bullying can be physical – such as hitting, pushing, pinching or stealing money. It can also be psychological – for example, teasing, name-calling, whispering, tale-telling and deliberately excluding people. There is a distinction between so-called 'ordinary' bullying and specific activities such as sexual or racial harassment, or homophobic bullying. The first type of bullying seems more individual, whereas the second is embedded within a culture that is patriarchal, institutionally racist and heterosexist. It is important to recognize these different types of bullying for two reasons.

First, they can have different effects on the victim.

For example, a child who is being teased because of something s/he said or did will suffer as a consequence, but the suffering caused to a child who is being taunted as a direct result of his/her ethnicity, gender, sexuality or because of any other characteristic that is a fundamental part of his/her identity, will be of a different nature, and may have more serious consequences for the child.

Second, anti-bullying strategies will depend on the type of bullying that is occurring. For example, specific strategies need to be used with children who verbally abuse and swear at other children if the verbal abuse is racist in nature.

All schools recognize the need to deal with bullies, and they use a wide range of strategies to ensure that incidents of bullying or harassment are reported, that perpetrators are dealt with effectively and that victims are given adequate support. The nature of these strategies will depend on the ethos of the school and the attitudes of the individual teachers concerned.

Real Life Application 6:
Social inclusion: pupil support

'Social inclusion: pupil support' is the title of a circular issued to schools by the Department for Education and Employment (1999). The circular sets out the legal position and examples of good practice relating to student behaviour and discipline and the use of exclusion. Exclusion of children from school is used particularly when the child is seriously disrupting the education of other children, or else is a threat to the safety of other children. In practice, children who repeatedly bully or harass their fellow students are often excluded.

The DfEE circular identifies specific groups of children who are more likely to be excluded from mainstream schools and an examination of this list sheds light on possible reasons for seriously disruptive behaviour, including bullying. Students at particular risk of exclusion include the following groups.

- **Black Caribbean students, especially boys:** the DfEE circular suggests that the higher rates of exclusion among black Caribbean boys could be a direct result of racism, either because the incidents that led to the boys' exclusion arose from racist harassment by other students, or because teachers stereotype black Caribbean boys or ignore cultural differences in manner and demeanour. Traveller children are also more likely to be excluded from school, and the same reasons may apply.

- **Children in care:** 'looked-after' children span the full ability range, but 75 per cent leave school with no qualifications; they have higher truancy and exclusion rates, and are more likely to become involved with crime or abusive situations after they leave school. A longitudinal study by Hodges and Tizard (1989) shows how children who are brought up in institutions can experience long-term difficulties in social interaction.

- **Children from families under stress:** home circumstances need to be taken into account when considering students' needs as unemployment, bereavement, the loss of a parent through divorce or separation and so on can all have an effect on children's emotional and educational development. There are many ways in which a child's family circumstances may lead him/her to bully or harass other children. Perhaps the child is suffering stress or abuse at home and 'takes it out' on a weaker classmate. If the child comes from a violent family, s/he may have learnt through the process of social learning (see Chapter 1, pages 7–8) that aggression can bring immediate rewards. Finally, it is possible that the child with a difficult home life is made to feel disempowered and helpless, and that bullying others is a way of creating an illusion of personal control. It is interesting to note that bullies have usually been bullied themselves, and this could lead to aggression and control becoming part of their social interaction.

- **Students entering school outside the normal year of entry:** students coming into a school mid-year have had their education disrupted and may have more difficulty in making friends. The difficulties faced by these students illustrates how social identity can create bullying. When a group of children pick on an individual, it may be as a way of reinforcing their own group identity or it may be scapegoating in which weaker individuals or minority groups are blamed and attacked for problems experienced by the majority.

Summary

- In 1999, the DfEE published a circular entitled 'Social inclusion: pupil support', which identified groups of students who were at particular risk of being excluded from mainstream schools.
- This list helps us to examine why some students exhibit the kinds of behaviour that are likely to get them excluded.

Questions

1 What does the list of the types of pupil more likely to be at risk of exclusion say about the causes of behaviour that leads to exclusion?

2 Drawing on your own school experience, what do you think is the most effective way of dealing with bullying in schools?

Attention-deficit hyperactivity disorder

Attention-deficit hyperactivity disorder (ADHD) affects about 3 per cent of the population, mostly male children, and is characterized by inattention, impulsiveness, poor concentration and hyperactivity. ADHD is a controversial diagnosis as researchers have so far failed to identify conclusively any physiological cause, although there is some evidence that it is linked to dopamine imbalances or frontal lobe dysfunction. As a result, ADHD is defined as a cluster of symptoms, but the fact that some of these symptoms seem to run in families suggests that ADHD may have a genetic cause, at least in part.

Children with ADHD appear to be very highly over-aroused, and it is possible that this is a chronic condition caused by physiological factors, such as allergic reactions to food additives, for example. A more common explanation is that these children are actually under-aroused and therefore constantly have to seek stimulation from the environment in order to prevent themselves becoming bored; this could account for the inability to concentrate on one thing for more than a few seconds, and the constant rushing around that is typical in children with ADHD. This last theory is supported by the fact that ADHD is often successfully treated with a drug called Ritalin – an amphetamine that increases psychological and physiological arousal, and, contrary to what might be expected, calms ADHD children down. However, Ritalin is a highly addictive substance and its use with small children is controversial.

Real Life Application 7:

Wonder drug or playground curse?

In an article that appeared in *The Guardian*, journalist Eileen Tracey writes:

[Ritalin] *is being prescribed in huge quantities as a cure for inattentive or difficult children: those with attention deficit disorder. But there are nasty side effects to Ritalin, not least of which is the fact that it is changing hands in the playground for money. Are the benefits of this addictive drug worth the consequences? Or are we just too lazy to find the real causes and cures of problem behaviour?*

The article starts off with the case of Tom, an A level student with a complete inability to concentrate on his work, who felt that his problems started because of lack of individual attention from teachers. Tom was prescribed Ritalin by a psychiatrist and the drug seemed to have a magic effect on his behaviour. Despite being classed in the USA as a Schedule II drug, alongside morphine and cocaine, Ritalin helps thousands of adults and children concentrate on activities more effectively. In 1998 in the UK, 92,000 NHS prescriptions were written for the drug and these figures seem set to double every year – and that's without including people who are being prescribed the drug privately or those taking other amphetamines as a treatment for ADHD. Side effects of Ritalin include anxiety, depression, aggression, insomnia and loss of appetite.

In 1999, a report by the Mental Health Foundation revealed that children are getting more and more stressed. Tracey suggests that Ritalin is being used as a cheap alternative to counselling and as a quick fix for reducing the number of school exclusions. She argues that there are many factors that could explain why so many children display the symptoms of ADHD – for example, junk food and additives, air pollution and violence on television. Children constantly receive instant gratification, but do not get the time to absorb information and grow up gently. Playtime is disappearing from schools, which are under increasing pressure to produce good test results. The divorce rate is soaring and this can affect children's behaviour at school. Tracey ends her article with the following paragraph:

Yes, Ritalin works. It enables our children to survive. It puts an end to the problem of too many questions. It stops us asking what message we give children when we give them drugs. It saves us thinking about why they can't learn, or focusing on an environment that makes them healthy and happy. It's our magic pill.

Article adapted from *The Guardian*, 12 October 1999

Summary

- Ritalin, an addictive amphetamine with unpleasant side-effects, is regularly prescribed to children with ADHD.
- Although Ritalin does have a positive effect on the behaviour of many such children, the author of the article in RLA 7 questions whether it is the best treatment for ADHD, or whether it is a way of suppressing the symptoms to avoid thinking about the root causes.

Questions

1 Explain why Ritalin removes some of the symptoms of ADHD.

2 Why might providing children with instant gratification lead to ADHD?

3 How might a behaviourist teacher deal with a child with ADHD?

School refusal

Many children play truant at some stage in their school careers and there are many reasons why an individual may choose not to go to school on a particular day. A child may want to avoid a particular lesson because s/he is likely to get into trouble with the teacher for some reason. Children may skip school to avoid another student, or because they need to stay at home to look after a younger sibling or simply because they've thought of something better to do. School refusers are children who repeatedly truant and are very difficult to persuade to attend school. There are several possible reasons why a child might develop a phobia of going to school.

- If the child's experience of school is very negative, maybe because they are constantly being bullied, or being made to feel stupid or inadequate in class, then skipping school could actually be more reinforcing than attending, despite the fact that the consequences of truancy are usually unpleasant.

- A child may have come to associate an unpleasant reaction with school; a traumatic experience, for example, could instil a phobia in the child – rather as Little Albert developed a phobia of white rats in the study by Watson and Rayner (see Key Study 1, page 2).
- The child could be suffering from separation anxiety. In other words, the child may be too insecure to leave a parent at home and be confident that s/he would still be there after school.
- The child might be suffering from serious depression, obsessive-compulsive disorder, or some other mental condition that makes it difficult for him/her to attend school.

Commentary

Some schools have attempted to 'bribe' students into attending regularly. For example, pupils at Firfield Community School in Newcastle were offered cash bonuses of £80 a term for turning up as part of a fresh start programme after it was failed by Ofsted in 1997, and the scheme appeared to be reducing truancy (*The Guardian*, 15 March 2000). An alternative to rewarding students for attending is to punish them for truanting. Every local education authority runs an education welfare service which has the legal responsibility to monitor attendance; if a child does not attend school regularly and if the parents fail to provide the school or the education welfare service with an acceptable explanation, they can be prosecuted in a Magistrates' court and fined up to £1,000. These behaviourist approaches, based on operant conditioning, may work for 'ordinary' truants, who are deciding not to go to school because they feel they benefit more from truanting. However, they may be less effective with school refusers, whose reasons for not attending school are more complex.

Classroom management

The preceding text described some specific examples of problem classroom behaviour and explored possible causes. Children with emotional or behavioural difficulties can be difficult to deal with, but low level 'naughtiness' can also be very disruptive in the classroom; teachers spend a great deal of time and effort attempting to 'control' their students. Humanist teachers argue that it is precisely these efforts to control children that encourage them to behave inappropriately. In his book on Summerhill School, the school's founder, AS Neill, says:

Neurosis begins with parental discipline – which is the very opposite of parental love. You cannot have a good humanity by treating it with hate and punishment and suppression. The only way is the way of love. A loving environment, without parental discipline, will take care of most of the troubles of childhood (Neill, 1960).

However, all teachers, including Neill, would agree that individual freedom should not extend to the freedom to hurt other people, and that it is necessary to maintain a classroom environment in which children can learn effectively. Teachers must take into account the needs and rights of individual students, but also those of the rest of the class. **Classroom management**, therefore, has two functions.

1 The facilitation of **learning**.
2 The prevention and correction of **misbehaviours**.

Teachers with different perspectives disagree how to fulfil these two functions, and even how to define them: 'learning' and 'misbehaviour' mean very different things to different people.

This text that follows examines behaviourist, humanist and cognitive techniques of classroom management. There are very few schools, such as Summerhill (see Chapter 1, pages 13–15), that attempt to focus exclusively on a single approach; in practice, a range of techniques is used in schools. However, individual teachers and schools use certain techniques more than others, and this depends on their general approach to education.

Behaviour modification

Behaviour modification is a set of behaviourist techniques based on operant conditioning and used to eliminate or change behaviour considered unacceptable by the teacher. The first step is to define this behaviour. This could consist of extreme behaviour, such as an individual child hitting other students, or more common behaviour, such as members of the class talking to each other when they should be working. Once this has been done, the teacher can consider the **antecedents** and **consequences** of the behaviour.

Antecedents

This refers to the conditions that apply immediately prior to the behaviour in question, and that may trigger, or even directly cause, the behaviour. If it is possible to change the antecedents of unwanted behaviour, then it could be prevented from occurring in the first place. For example, if a class tends to lose concentration, and the teacher notices that this happens immediately after a certain event (such as asking one of the students to read from the textbook), then the teacher could avoid this.

Changing the antecedents of behaviour is not, strictly speaking, an aspect of operant conditioning because Skinner's theory focuses entirely on the consequences of actions (see pages 3–4). However, this has become an important aspect of modern behavioural techniques and is in line with the general philosophy of behaviourism as it does not really question the root causes of behaviour or examine internal mental processes. For example, if a certain child seems to become aggressive in class every time s/he is asked to hand out worksheets, then the behaviourist teacher is content to avoid asking that child to perform that particular task – as long as it stops the child becoming aggressive – and is not overly concerned with the reasons behind the aggression.

Behaviour
This is the specific behaviour that the teacher wishes to change or eliminate.

Consequences
This refers to the outcome of the behaviour for the children concerned. The theory of operant conditioning suggests that children will only continue to behave in certain ways if they receive reinforcement for doing so. It is therefore important to make sure that children are reinforced for wanted behaviour, and not reinforced for unwanted behaviour. The most common way in which 'bad' behaviour is reinforced in the classroom is by **attention**, either from the teacher or from other students, and it is often the case that a particular child will prefer negative attention (for example, being told off) to no attention.

Other ways in which bad behaviour can be rewarded are, for example, by being sent out of the classroom (some children might find this a relief) or by receiving recognition and admiration from other students. There are several ways in which teachers can influence the consequences of behaviour in order to modify it.

- **They can make sure that students do not receive reinforcement for 'bad' behaviour:** this usually consists of ignoring children when they are naughty and rewarding them when they are good. It is also important to make sure that children are not deriving any other hidden benefit from punishment. It is more difficult to ensure

that a child does not receive the admiration of his/her fellow students by challenging the teacher, but this is a function of the ethos that exists in the classroom to begin with. If there is an 'us and them' atmosphere in which the students feel generally antagonistic to the teacher, then it is more likely that they will admire anyone who confronts the teacher.

- **They can punish children for 'bad' behaviour:** apart from a few extreme humanist schools, some form of punishment or sanction takes place in every classroom in the world. However, there are practical problems associated with punishment, and these are discussed on pages 6, 13. Some teachers argue that, as well as being ineffective in teaching children 'good' behaviour, punishment is ethically wrong in the sense that it is a breach of basic human rights for any one person to impose his or her will on another by the use of sanctions. In practice, although punishment may well be harmful in many ways and ineffective in bringing about long-term behaviour change, the reason it is used so frequently in classrooms is because it is a very quick and easy way to get children to do what the teacher wants them to do immediately.

- **They can reward children for 'good' behaviour:** for a detailed discussion of how behaviourists attempt to change children's behaviour by offering extrinsic reinforcers of different kinds, see Chapter 1 (pages 5–8).

When behaviour modification is used in a clinical setting, psychologists observe and record the behaviour in question, as well as the antecedents and consequences. They will design a systematic programme for altering the antecedents or consequences and will measure the behaviour before and after the intervention in order to ascertain its effectiveness. When behaviour modification occurs in the classroom, it is rarely this systematic; a teacher with 30 or more students simply cannot make detailed observations of a single child. However, teachers do apply behaviour modification in a more ad hoc manner, and it can be a very effective technique for making children behave differently.

Commentary

- A common criticism of behaviour modification is that it is the teacher who decides which behaviour is 'good' or 'bad' and **manipulates** the student into changing, almost without his or her consent. It is much better if the teacher is able to reason with the student, and get him or her to agree that the behaviour is question is unacceptable (see the description of cognitive behaviour therapy below). In practice, however, this is not always possible, and when students do agree that they should not be acting in a certain way, they may only be doing so in order to get out of trouble. However, there is some degree of consensus among teachers, parents and students, as to which behaviours are unacceptable in the classroom and maybe behaviour modification techniques should be restricted to these.

- The negative effects of punishment are listed below.

1 Punishment draws attention to unwanted behaviour: by punishing children for doing something wrong rather than rewarding them for behaving well, teachers focus the attention of the class on the 'bad' behaviour.

2 Punishment is accompanied by negative emotional side-effects: children who are punished may feel angry and resentful, especially if they feel that the punishment is undeserved. They may also internalize the punishment and experience lower self-esteem. Finally, punishment damages the relationship between student and teacher.

3 Punishment often suppresses behaviour rather than eliminating it: children develop strategies for avoiding punishment rather than learning that the behaviour that instigated the punishment is wrong. In behaviourist terms, if children lie in order to avoid punishment, for example, then they receive reinforcement for an anti-social behaviour.

4 Punishment provides children with harmful messages: as the 'victims' of punishment, children receive a clear object lesson that strength and power are effective ways of getting other people to do what you want.

- In order to avoid punishment, teachers who use behaviour modification must concentrate entirely on ignoring unwanted behaviour, and reinforcing wanted behaviour. However, this raises two problems.

1 Bad behaviour can sometimes be very difficult to ignore, especially if it is causing serious disruption to the class or putting other people in danger. By ignoring a student's behaviour, it is hoped that s/he will stop it because there is no reinforcement forthcoming. It is always possible that the student will simply escalate the behaviour and become more demanding. If the teacher eventually gives in and tells the student off, then s/he learns that persisting with the bad behaviour is effective in gaining the teacher's attention (see the text on partial reinforcement which appears in Chapter 1, page 5).

2 In extreme cases, the child rarely, or never, exhibits the wanted behaviour and so the teacher is unable to provide appropriate reinforcement. There are two techniques for dealing with this situation. First, in **behaviour shaping** the teacher does not wait until the child displays the wanted behaviour in full, but reinforces successive approximations to that behaviour. For example, if a teacher wishes a child with ADHD to sit quietly at a table and draw a picture, s/he may have to wait forever until the child does this. However, if s/he first of all provides reinforcement when the child stops running around the classroom, then when s/he sits down, then picks up the pencil and so on, the child will gradually be encouraged to do what the teacher wants. The second technique is to use **non-contingent reinforcement**. This is a recently developed technique in which the child is systematically rewarded at fixed time intervals, whether s/he has displayed the required behaviour or not. This works because it creates a **flooding effect** in which the child learns that reinforcement does not only come when s/he behaves badly. After a time, the reinforcement is slightly delayed when the child displays the unwanted behaviour; the programme now resembles traditional operant conditioning more closely. Humanists might argue that non-contingent reinforcement does not work because of behaviourist learning theory, but because the unconditional positive regard it represents makes the child feel valued and less willing to engage in anti-social behaviour.

Cognitive behaviour therapy

The criticism that cognitive psychologists may make about the traditional behaviourist approach to classroom control is that it takes no account of the child's thought processes. In fact, it is hard to accept that children do not think about what is happening to them when a teacher attempts to use a behaviourist technique to alter their behaviour; it can be argued that when a child acts differently as a result of a behaviour modification programme, s/he realizes exactly what the teacher is trying to do and has decided to comply for rational reasons.

Cognitive behaviour therapy (CBT) is based on the assumption that children's behaviour in the classroom relates to their interpretations of events and not, as traditional behaviourists would argue, simply to the events themselves (that is, what we think is fundamentally important to what we do). Our interpretation of events is linked to our beliefs about ourselves and about the world around us: if these beliefs are irrational or deluded, then our behaviour is flawed. For example, if a child thinks that everybody in the class hates him or her, then s/he may become hostile and aggressive. Cognitive therapies attempt to challenge irrational beliefs by, for example, reminding the child mentioned above of interactions with classmates in which it was clear that they did not hate him or her. The underlying theory of CBT is not so very different from that of traditional operant conditioning; people still behave in ways which provide reinforcement but whether the outcomes, or predicted outcomes, of a particular action are perceived as reinforcement depends on their cognitive appraisal of the situation.

Teachers use informal cognitive behaviour therapy all the time in the classroom, in the sense that they constantly challenge students' opinions and beliefs, and try to persuade them to accept certain values. More formal programmes are very time consuming and beyond the scope of most teachers. A specific example of a cognitive programme is described in Key Study 5 (see below).

KEY STUDY 5

Researchers: Meichenbaum and Goodman (1971)

Aim: To demonstrate the effectiveness of a cognitive behavioural intervention (**self-instructional training**) in treating impulsive and hyperactive children (see text on ADHD, pages 42–43)

Method: Fifteen children placed in a special education classroom because of behavioural problems (hyperactivity and poor self-control) were split into three groups of five. The first group (SI) received the self-instructional treatment, the second (attention-control) did not receive any treatment but were given an equivalent amount of attention, and the third (assessment-control) received no treatment or attention and were used to establish a baseline. The self-instructional training programme consisted of four hours and 30 minutes spread over two weeks, during which the following procedures were carried out.

1 The researcher performed a task while talking through it out loud – the child observed.
2 The child performed the same task while the researcher gave instructions out loud.
3 The child performed the task, speaking self-instructions out loud.
4 The child performed the task, whispering self-instructions.
5 The child performed the task by thinking the self-instructions to him/herself.

The SI group were instructed in this way to perform a range of sensory-motor and problem-solving tasks.

Results: The SI group performed significantly better on the tasks than the children in the two control groups immediately and when they were re-assessed three weeks later. Unfortunately, there was no observable improvement in classroom behaviour or in teacher ratings of behaviour for these children.

Conclusions: Meichenbaum and Goodman concluded that a cognitive self-instructional programme that teaches children to talk to themselves can help impulsive or hyperactive children to concentrate on their work and that this, eventually, will have beneficial effects on their classroom behaviour.

The humanist approach to classroom management

In general, the humanist approach to classroom management is **preventative** rather than **corrective**. In other words, the humanist teacher will try to promote an ethos in the classroom that will make it easier for children to behave in ways that are conducive to learning. For example, by valuing and respecting children, by refusing to mistreat or oppress them, and by allowing them freedom of action and expression, the humanist hopes that the children's natural goodness and curiosity will shine through. In this way, children will not only be keen to engage in education for its own sake, but will also treat each other, and the teachers, with love and respect.

This is not to say that humanists do not have strategies to deal with behaviour problems in the classroom, but these strategies tend to be much more democratic than those employed by behaviourist teachers. Webster (1968; cited in LeFrançois, 1997), for example, describes a set of procedures by which democratic order can be maintained in the classroom.

- Teachers must make sure that all the students understand what the rules are *and the reasons for their existence*.
- The first violation of a rule should lead to a warning, a discussion of alternative ways of behaving and clarification of the consequences of repeated infractions.
- Teachers should endeavour to discover the underlying causes of misbehaviour.
- Whenever possible, teachers should address students in private regarding their misbehaviour.
- Sarcasm, ridicule and other forms of discipline that lead to public humiliation should be avoided.
- Teachers should apologize when they make mistakes.
- The punishment should fit the crime; minor misbehaviours should not bring about harsh punishment.
- Extra class work an assignments, tests and other school-related activities should never be used as a form of punishment.

These principles are put into practice at Summerhill School; AS Neill (1960) describes it as a self-governing school in which all punishment for social offences is settled by vote at weekly school meetings. All children and staff have an equal say in deciding what the school rules should be and what to do if anyone breaks them. Few schools are this democratic, but similar principles can be used in 'ordinary' schools to a certain degree. Even within a particular school, some teachers will act in a more democratic way than others. Humanist techniques of classroom management are sometimes referred to as **conflict management** or **pro-social programmes**, and a specific example of such a programme is described in RLA 8 (below).

Real Life Application 8:
Fostering pro-social behaviour

Moreno and Torrego (1999) carried out two case studies in Spain – one in a primary and one in a secondary school. In each case, the researchers first gathered data on the nature and extent of anti-social behaviour in the two schools, then helped the teachers to instigate a programme designed to improve the level of pro-social behaviour. The two schools chosen for this study were both state-run schools near Madrid. The schools volunteered to take part in the study and both were already supposed to deliver good practice regarding the prevention of anti-social behaviour. The whole study took place over a six-month period (from January to June 1998).

The researchers started by initiating a school self-review process in which the teachers identified anti-social behaviour within the school; they came up with behaviours such as lack of discipline (breaking school/classroom rules), bullying, vandalism, physical violence (aggression, extortion, use of weapons), sexual harassment, absenteeism and fraud (examination cheating, plagiarism, abuse of personal connections and so on). The next step was, alongside the teachers, to plan and implement a set of solutions designed to deal with the anti-social behaviours that had been identified.

1 Extend and deepen knowledge about the students so that a more personalized educational response can be given (especially for students at risk).
2 Introduce changes in the school curriculum, making it more inclusive and democratic. Emphasize the teaching and learning of democratic values (tolerance, respect, solidarity, co-operation and so on).
3 Stimulate and develop the classroom student

group (especially by focusing on the rules of behaviour in the classroom, rather than the overall school's code of behaviour).

4 Promote a higher level of family support to both students and teachers (by working with students' families and introducing training activities for parents).

5 Encourage social and community influences on students' behaviour (for example, youth groups, sports clubs, churches, and volunteer associations).

6 Review and improve teachers' classroom management skills (verbal and non-verbal interaction, teachers' discourse, motivational style and immediate reaction to disruption).

7 Develop in all members of the school community inter-personal communication skills and methods of democratic conflict resolution.

8 Create structures at the school's institutional level to promote a more rational and healthy daily coexistence (for example, committees, mediation groups, student 'ombudsman' associations, voluntary activities and campaigns).

9 Work with the school's code of behaviour (discussing the setting of rules, procedures for the enforcing of rules and procedures to follow when rules are broken).

10 Introduce specific measures to face and deal with cases of extreme violence.

After six months of work in the two schools, Moreno and Torrego concluded the following.

- The most positive achievement of the programme was that the teachers recognized the importance of pro-social education and valued the fact that they 'discovered' the deep social and cultural roots of anti-social behaviour.
- On the other hand, there was some resistance among teachers to the programme (for example, dismissing the programme as too theoretical for use in a real classroom). The researchers noticed that personal problems among the teachers themselves could lead them to ignore students' anti-social behaviour and its effects.
- It became clear that eliminating old classroom practices was as important as introducing new ones; some of the teachers became aware that the violence that the school system and individual teachers exert on students may contribute to their anti-social behaviour. The need to discard many deeply rooted practices became a highly controversial issue in both schools.
- Preventative measures were seen by teachers as

effective in dealing with anti-social behaviour, but only in the long run. Therefore, a plan of preventative actions should not completely neglect the need for corrective action in the short term.

Summary

- This study, by Moreno and Torrego, involved the teachers in two schools in a process of review and development aimed at promoting pro-social behaviours.
- A range of 'solutions' were introduced, largely based on humanist principles.
- These solutions were successful in some ways, but their implementation raised certain issues amongst teachers in the schools.

Questions

1 In what ways are the ten solutions described in RLA 8 humanist in approach?

2 Was Moreno and Torrego's research a 'success'?

3 To what extent are solutions such as these used in mainstream schools in the UK nowadays?

Real Life Application 9:
How to be a good teacher

In his book *Psychology for Teachers*, Fontana (1995) sets out a number of practical hints and tips for teachers, drawing together behaviourist, cognitive and humanist principles.

1 **Interest the class:** a class that is absorbed in its work will not want to cause problems; teachers need to provide work that is relevant, interesting and enjoyable to students.

2 **Avoid personal mannerisms:** unusual mannerisms of speech and dress can seem irritating or comic to children.

3 **Be fair:** be consistent, make the punishment match the offence.

4 **Be humorous:** be prepared to introduce humour into teaching material, to laugh at yourself, and

and to laugh with the class (but not at the expense of other students).

5 **Avoid unnecessary threats:** threats are not a particularly good way of controlling children, but issuing threats and then failing to carry them out can seriously undermine the teacher's position.

6 **Be punctual:** in order to set a good example, and also so that the class does not get out of hand before you set foot in the classroom.

7 **Avoid anger:** if you lose your temper in the classroom, you may say things you regret later. Students may take advantage of your loss of self-control.

8 **Avoid over-familiarity:** be friendly, but not too familiar, as this confuses children who know that the teacher represents school authority.

9 **Offer opportunities for responsibility:** offering children responsibility shows them that they have the teacher's confidence and also helps them to take some responsibility for what happens in the classroom.

10 **Focus attention:** it is more effective to ask a child by name to be quiet, rather than to address the class as a whole; another advantage of learning your students' names as quickly as possible is that it demonstrates your interest in them as individuals.

11 **Avoid humiliating children:** this can not only harm the 'victims', but also turn the rest of the class against the teacher.

12 **Be alert:** try to know what is happening at all times in every part of the classroom.

13 **Use positive language:** explain to children what you want them to do, rather than what they should not do.

14 **Be confident:** teaching involves quite a lot of bluff on the part of the teacher; teachers with a hesitant or tentative manner give children the impression that they are expecting trouble (see RLA 4, pages 26–27, on the self-fulfilling prophecy).

15 **Be well-organized:** a well-organized lesson is less likely to be disrupted by misbehaviour than one in which the worksheets contain mistakes or the video recorder does not work.

16 **Show that you like children:** teachers who are able to convey messages of sympathy, understanding and a personal delight in the job of teaching children tend to have fewer behavioural problems to deal with in the classroom.

Summary

• Fontana describes a set of tips for teachers in order to improve classroom practice; these are based on behaviourist, humanist and cognitive approaches.

Questions

1 For each of the suggestions given in RLA 9, explain why it works and determine whether it is based on a behaviourist, cognitive or humanist approach to classroom management.

The classroom environment

In this chapter we have so far examined problem behaviours and the techniques that teachers use to manage them. Another key factor that influences learning in schools is the physical classroom environment. **Environmental psychologists** have carried out a great deal of research to discover how the classroom setting can facilitate or hinder learning, but there is a recognition that there is no universal answer to this question. A particular classroom layout, for example, may suit a specific teaching style and different subjects are best taught in different types of classroom. The text that follows first discusses classroom layout (that is, the way the tables are placed and what is put on the walls), then considers briefly other environmental factors such as noise, temperature, light and colour.

Classroom layout

Traditionally designed classrooms have the desks laid out in rows, with the teacher's desk at the front of the classroom, sometimes on a raised platform. This is an efficient way of filling a room as less space is wasted between desks. Also, the students are all facing the teacher, rather than each other, and they can all see the board at the front of the room. This design is suited to authoritarian, didactic teaching and still exists in many schools today. However, there is contradictory evidence as to whether this is the best way of setting out desks in a classroom (see Key Studies 6 and 7, pages 51–52).

KEY STUDY 6

Researchers: Wheldall *et al* (1981)

Aim: To compare the effect of classroom seating arrangements (in rows or around tables) on children's 'on-task' behaviour.

Method: Two mixed-ability classes from different schools in the UK, containing children aged 10 and 11, where seating was normally around tables, were systematically observed for two weeks in their usual 'tables' seating arrangement, followed by a further two weeks seated in rows, and finally for another two weeks seated around tables. The classes were observed daily by two independent observers for 30 to 40 minutes during academic lessons. Using a stopwatch and pre-prepared sheet, each child was observed and rated every 5 seconds as to whether s/he had been 'on-task' for the whole of the preceding 5 seconds or not. 'On-task' behaviour was defined as compliance with teacher instructions, eye contact with the teacher when requested, eye contact with textbooks and materials when asked to get on with set work. 'Off-task' behaviour included calling out, interrupting a neighbour, talking to a neighbour, being out of one's seat without permission, non-compliance with teacher instructions and not getting on with the set work.

Results: The inter-observer agreement was around 90 per cent, supporting the reliability of the measures obtained. For both classes, mean on-task behaviour was higher when the children were placed in rows then when they were seated around tables. The rows condition had its most powerful effect on children with low initial on-task behaviour. Overall, on-task behaviour was lower in the final

tables condition than in the initial one. After the study was carried out, the children said that they preferred sitting in rows, and the teachers of both classes opted for a permanent change to rows.

Conclusions: Children pay more attention in class when they are seated in rows.

KEY STUDY 7

Researchers: Rosenfield *et al* (1985)

Aim: To compare the effect of three types of classroom arrangement (rows, clusters and circles) on observed student behaviour.

Method: From six fifth and sixth grade classes in elementary schools in California, three were selected for the experimental conditions, in which desk arrangements were varied. The remaining three classes were identified as control groups (that is, each was assigned one of the three different classroom layouts). In each of the six classes, eight students (four boys and four girls) were selected to be observed: two high ability and two low ability, two high interactors (that is, high verbal participation in class discussion) and two low interactors. The three classroom arrangements used were rows, clusters (desks arranged in groups of up to eight) and circles (all the desks in a large circle). The three experimental classes tried these three arrangements in varying orders. The three control classes each tried a different arrangement; the purpose of the control classes was to compare observed behaviour in two classrooms with the same arrangement, in order to rule out confounding variables caused by teacher style. Each classroom observation sequence for each desk arrangement consisted of three 20-minute

	lessons, broken down into twenty 60-second observation periods. Students were observed while brainstorming ideas for writing assignments and their behaviour was categorized as on-task (hand-raising, making relevant comments, listening) or off-task (disruptive behaviour, withdrawal).
Results:	Students seated in clusters engaged in significantly more on-task behaviour than those in rows, but not as much as those in circles. The different categories of students were observed to behave differently from each other, but no significant interaction between ability, level of interaction and classroom arrangement was found.
Conclusions:	Desks arranged in circles and, to a lesser extent, in clusters, during classroom discussion can facilitate interaction as well as diminish off-task behaviour.

Key studies 6 and 7 seem contradictory but, apart from the fact that each of them has certain methodological problems and that different teachers will define 'on-task' and 'off-task' behaviour quite differently, together they reinforce the notion that the most effective classroom layout depends on the type of lesson being taught and the style of the teacher. For example, if a teacher is trying to encourage children to take part in discovery learning (see Chapter 2, page 31), then an **open classroom** arrangement, in which students are free to move about, use available resources and work together in groups, may be most suitable. On the other hand, for didactic teaching, sitting the students in rows is probably the best way of keeping their attention. Finally, if the teacher wishes to hold a class discussion, the advantage of putting desks in a circle is that every student can see and interact with every other.

Another aspect of classroom layout, apart from the way the desks are arranged, is how much and what kinds of material are put on the walls. Creekmore (1987; cited in Gifford, 1997) argues that each classroom should contain three different types of walls.

- **Acquisition wall:** this should be placed at the front of the room and should hold the blackboard/whiteboard and the class notice-board. Only material relating to educational concepts that are new or that students are struggling with should be placed on this wall.
- **Maintenance walls:** these should be at the sides of the room, and should help students review and understand more fully material with which they are already familiar.
- **Dynamic wall:** this should be at the back of the room and should contain students' work, temporary notices, holiday decorations and so on.

Creekmore's (1987) rationale is that this distribution of different learning materials around the classroom enables students to focus their attention without interference.

A second issue relating to wall displays is how much to include. The humanist teacher would argue that complex and informative wall displays create a rich environment which facilitates the process of discovery learning. Furthermore, presenting students' work on the walls can have a positive effect on self-esteem (as long as this is done in a non-competitive way) and can help children work co-operatively. More didactic teachers, on the other hand, may consider complex wall displays to be distracting to students and therefore make it more difficult for them to concentrate on their studies. There is little research that compares sparse wall displays with more complex ones, but as with the question of desk layout, it seems likely that the best way of decorating classroom walls depends on the style of the teacher and the subject being taught in that classroom.

Commentary

Different types of classroom layout are more suitable to different teaching styles, and it is important that teachers make sure that these match up. For example, it may be counterproductive to attempt to teach a didactic lesson when the students are sitting round tables, some with their backs to the teacher, or to set the children some individual work when they are sitting in groups in which they can distract each other. Similarly, it is hard for children sitting in rows to engage in whole-class discussion. Ideally, the layout of a particular classroom should be flexible to allow for different types of lessons, but this is difficult to achieve in practice and it is probably the case that many lessons are taught in classrooms that are laid out inappropriately.

Noise

Most teachers assume that noise in the classroom hinders learning and spend a lot of effort attempting to keep noise levels low so that students can concentrate better. However, the relationship between noise in the classroom and students' performance is not straightforward. For example, different students react to noise in different ways depending on individual characteristics such as gender, motivation, personality, ability and so on. Noise can have an adverse effect on performance on certain types of task and actually enhance performance on others. Different types of noise have different effects (noise tends to be more distracting if it is loud, unpredictable and uncontrollable). Finally, noise has a different effect if it occurs during the learning of material or during the task performance. There has been a great deal of research on the effects of noise on performance as the examples that follow show.

- **Bronzaft (1981):** the reading ability of children in a New York School was measured and found to be significantly lower for those who had classrooms on the side of the building facing a noisy train line. One year after rubber sound-reducing materials were installed on the train line, this difference had disappeared.
- **Cohen et al (1981):** the mathematics and reading achievement of third graders in an area of Los Angeles that has aeroplanes flying overhead every 2 minutes 30 seconds was found to be significantly lower than that of children in schools that were not in the flight path, or that had sound insulation installed in their classrooms.
- **Christie and Glickman (1980):** elementary school children were given visual puzzles to do in noisy and in quiet conditions. Overall, there was no difference in performance between the conditions, but the boys did significantly better when it was noisy, and the girls did better when it was quiet.
- **Zentall (1983):** this study showed that noisy rock music actually helped hyperactive children to be less disruptive and verbally aggressive, but made autistic children more passive and repetitive in their actions than usual.
- **Cohen et al (1973):** children who lived in a block of apartments, built near a busy road, were tested on their reading ability. All the children were tested in quiet conditions, but those who lived in the noisier apartments achieved lower scores, indicating that the effects of noise can outlast the noise itself.

There are several reasons why noise may have an adverse affect on the learning process. Perhaps it interferes with communication between students and teacher or among students. It may interfere with cognitive processes such as memory or problem-solving. Finally, it may cause stress or lower students' sense of personal control.

Commentary

As mentioned above, teachers recognize that too much noise is bad for learning, but how much noise is too much? Teachers have to be careful that they do not stifle educationally useful interaction among students in order to maintain a quiet and apparently orderly classroom. Lessons involving group work or discovery learning, for example, are likely to be noisier than ones in which the students are supposed to be working on their own or listening to the teacher.

Temperature

If we widen the issue of classroom temperature to include other climate factors such as humidity and air circulation, there is evidence that this can affect learning. In most schools, climate is fairly well controlled, but classrooms can be too hot in summer (or even in winter if the heating is high and there is little ventilation), or too cold or damp. An interesting aspect of research in this area is that it is not always the case that the climate that makes students most comfortable is the one at which they perform at an optimal level. Again, without going into details of specific studies, it seems that children perform better in arithmetic or general intelligence tests and at language tasks when the temperature is slightly lower than they normally find comfortable, and when humidity is low and air circulation high. In PE lessons, higher temperatures are associated with lower performance and fitness. Students in hot climates perform better if the classrooms are air-conditioned. In general, it seems that cooler and less humid classrooms are better for learning but, again, it is likely that individual students perform better in climates they prefer or are more used to.

Light and colour

There are several questions to consider in determining the best kind of lighting to have in a classroom. Most classrooms in the UK use fluorescent lighting, but is daylight, or at least artificial lighting that simulates daylight, better? What is the effect on students of light reflecting off surfaces in the classroom? What is the optimum intensity of light, and is this the same for everyone or does each individual perform better at the level of brightness that s/he prefers? Linked to the issue of lighting is that of colour. Most primary school classrooms contain bright colours, whereas secondary classrooms tend to be painted in more pastel shades. Does the colour of the walls actually make any difference to the learning process?

There have been several research studies aimed at answering these kinds of question, and, without quoting any specific ones, below is a summary of some of the findings.

- Students and teachers tend to prefer 'ordinary' light bulbs to fluorescent lighting, but fluorescent lights are much cheaper and have not been shown to affect either the performance or the health of students in any significant way.

- Although a minimum of light intensity is required for students to see what they are doing, the human eye is very adaptable to different lighting levels and there does not seem to be an overall association between intensity of illumination (within the range found in classrooms in practice) and performance, although it may be the case that specific children prefer certain levels of lighting and work best when they are provided in their classrooms.

- Environmental psychologists, perhaps surprisingly, have not really found that the colour of the walls in a classroom affects performance or mental state to any significant degree. Many people believe that emotional arousal can be affected by colour; for example, red is supposed to make people more angry and blue more calm. Research has failed to discover any changes in physiological arousal as a result of working in differently coloured rooms, but it may be that a red room makes those in it feel more excitable or angry, or a blue room calmer and more passive, simply because we think it should do. Of course, it may be that students work better in rooms that are painted in their own favourite colour, but this is an individual preference and does not lead to any generalizations about the 'best' colour to paint a classroom.

Commentary

The fact that psychologists have found little evidence that type or intensity of lighting or wall colour has any impact on student performance or behaviour may hide a large effect of these factors on individual students or even groups of students. In other words, in general, light and colour seem irrelevant for students as a whole, but they may have a large impact on a few people.

Real Life Application 10:
The soft classroom

A paper by Sommer and Olsen (1980) describes a successful attempt to design and implement an alternative classroom at the University of California. Previous classrooms were very traditional, with the chairs arranged in straight rows facing the front of the room, or around a large rectangular table in the smaller seminar rooms. Students rated these rooms as cold, impersonal, bare and ugly. Furthermore, little student interaction occurred in the classrooms. Even in the seminar rooms, student comments only took up about six minutes of a one-hour session; the rest of the time was taken up by the teacher. In the lecture rooms, there was no interaction among students (except for whispering between students sitting next to each other); it was as if the desks being in rows gave the message to the students that all interaction should be between student and teacher, and not among students.

At first, Sommer and Olsen attempted to improve the classrooms by bringing in plants, putting up posters and mobiles and even painting a mural. These small changes were well received but when they attempted to put the desks in a large circle instead of in rows, the students moved them back before the class started. At this point, the researchers asked for permission from the university to redesign one of the classrooms completely and received a modest grant to pay for the changes. During the next month, they carried out an extensive survey of staff and students to discover opinions about lighting, furniture and so on. During the summer of 1974, the classroom was remodelled. It started off with 30 chairs with attached writing surfaces facing two large tables and a teacher's chair at the front of the room. This was replaced with sofas and cushions around the edges of the room, a small blackboard and a multi-coloured carpet. Lighting could be controlled using a dimmer switch, wooden panels were used to break up the rectangular shape of the room, and decorative coat hooks and mobiles were put up.

The researchers were worried that the new classroom would be vandalized or misused in some way, and posted observers to keep an eye on it and to record people's reactions. Students and staff were very positive about the room and students participated to a much greater degree in lessons (about three times as much as when the desks were in rows). They also moved about the room during lessons. The fact that there was no focal point where the teacher should stand meant that s/he could also move around, creating a more informal, democratic environment.

Some classes were not suited to the room because they were too large or required specialist equipment. Also, the researchers had trouble persuading site staff to maintain the room properly. There was no equipment available for vacuuming the carpet and, interestingly, the male site staff considered jobs such as vacuuming, rearranging sofa cushions and watering plants as 'women's work', whereas they were much more willing to carry out traditional jobs such as fastening rows of chairs together or polishing tiled floors with heavy machines.

The creation of a 'soft classroom' may not seem particularly revolutionary nowadays, but Sommer and Olsen felt they were breaking new ground in classroom design. They considered their experiment a success in that the new classroom was much preferred by the large majority of students and staff, and that it did a great deal to encourage student participation in lessons.

Summary

• In 1974, Sommer and Olsen overcame practical difficulties to build a 'soft classroom' at the University of California.

• The furnishings and design of the soft classroom were intended to improve the relationships between teacher and students, and among students.
• The new design was successful, and was liked by both staff and students; some of the ideas contained within the soft classroom have been adopted in classroom design since.

Questions

1 What are the advantages and disadvantages of the soft classroom?

2 What age groups of learners might benefit most from a soft classroom and why?

3 To what extent have the principles of the soft classroom been incorporated into classroom design in the UK?

Example essay questions

1 Describe and evaluate commonly used psychological techniques used to control children with behaviour problems.

2 Suggest strategies aimed at preventing behaviour problems from occurring in (a) a primary school, (b) a secondary school and (c) a sixth form.

3 Based on psychological evidence, suggest suitable designs for (a) a primary school classroom, (b) a library in a secondary school and (c) a classroom for teaching sixth formers.

The soft classroom

4 Factors affecting learning

This chapter describes how gender, ethnicity and class affect learning, then goes on to examine a number of explanations of why this happens. The final two sections consider different types of special needs (including giftedness) and discuss ways of meeting them in the classroom. In particular, arguments are set out in favour of, and against, integrating children with special needs into mainstream classrooms. Real Life Applications that are considered are:

- RLA 11: Anti-racist education
- RLA 12: Boys' underachievement? Not the real question
- RLA 13: Research puts dyslexia test on new footing
- RLA 14: Inclusive education is a 'human right'
- RLA 15: Scared of becoming a gifted outcast
- RLA 16: Growing gifted children in the desert.

It is widely known that not all students do equally well in the school environment, and a great deal of research has been carried out into the reasons why this might be so. In particular, there appear to be marked differences in the performance of certain groups of students when they are compared to others. Examples of these are considered throughout this chapter.

Cultural factors

There are differences in the performance of boys compared to girls. There are also differences in the performance of students of different social classes within our society, as well as between the performance of different ethnic groups, and we will look at these three areas of difference in the text that follows.

There are many possible influences on the educational attainment of individual students and of particular groups of students. The explanations can be grouped in terms of where the influences are seen to come from. There are many theories that focus on environmental influences from outside the school, and many theories that focus on influences that come from within the school itself. More controversially there are also explanations that focus on biological differences, particularly in relation to the differences in the performance of boys and girls.

Gender

Gender differences in educational attainment are interesting because they are not static. For many years boys outperformed girls (especially in exam results) at most levels of the educational system, but in recent years the balance has shifted in favour of girls in many areas.

In terms of gender difference in educational attainment, biological explanations, the environment and the school as possible sources of influence will be examined. It is useful, first, to look at the more traditional explanations of gender differences in the education system, then study the recent success of girls and possible explanations for this.

The influence of biological differences

Some theorists argue that there are biological differences between boys and girls that can explain the different levels of attainment between them in school. For example, it is thought that girls mature earlier than boys and this may account for some of the reasons why girls do better than boys in school up to the age of about eleven.

Gray and Buffrey (1971) argue that girls and boys develop different aptitudes after the age of two, based on the dominance of different hemispheres of the brain. They argue that this is due to the influence of hormones on the brain, which explains why boys show a greater aptitude for spatial and mathematical tasks in primary school (associated with the right hemisphere) and girls show a greater aptitude for verbal reasoning tasks (associated with the left hemisphere). Halpern (1992; cited in Golombok and Fivush, 1994) also argues that hormones are important and that certain levels of testosterone are necessary to produce good spatial skills.

Commentary

- These explanations are problematic, however, because there are so many other possible reasons for the differences in performance, that the biological evidence, whatever it may be, is inconclusive. It cannot be denied that there are biological differences between boys and girls, but whether these can account for differences in their educational performance is another thing. It is just as likely that the way in which children are socialized (brought up) might have an influence. For example, the type of toys that boys play with when they are young may have an influence on their ability to perform visuo–spatial tasks when they go to school; and the types of activities that girls are encouraged to engage in might influence their verbal reasoning.
- Hyde *et al* (1990), who examined more than 100 research studies of gender difference, have also shown that any gender differences in spatial, mathematical and reasoning tasks are very small. They also show that these small differences have been decreasing over the last two decades; suggesting that socialization must at least play a part.

The influence of the environment on gender differences
Environmental differences can be looked at in terms of socialization within the home, and the influence of peers and the media on gender differences.

By the time girls and boys go to school at the age of four their experiences at home and with their peers will have shaped their attitudes to gender roles to a considerable degree. Pilcher (1999) agues that 'doing gender', as she calls it, is learnt from toys, books, clothing and television. She states that:

[G]irls and boys enter the formal education system looking and behaving in 'gender-appropriate' ways and with their own firmly held expectations and understandings about the differences between girls and women on the one hand and boys and men on the other (1999, p. 17).

Parental expectations, and the ways in which girls and boys are socialized by their parents, may have a considerable influence on their behaviour in the classroom. Some research suggests that parents still have different expectations of boys and girls, and that these stereotyped expectations may affect their children. For example, Lummis and Stevenson (1990) showed that parents expected their daughters to be good at reading and their sons to be good at maths.

Yee and Eccles (1988; cited by Golombok and Fivush, 1994) asked the parents of children to answer questions on their children's ability in maths. There were no gender differences in the ability of the children; however, the mothers of girls thought their daughters were less able at maths than the mothers of boys. The mothers also thought that their daughters had to work harder than their sons to achieve good grades in maths, and fathers also showed the same attitudes. Yee and Eccles argue that this is important because they suggest that girls are learning (from their parents) to make different attributions for their achievements. Girls are learning that their success is due to hard work, whereas boys are learning that their success is due to their own ability.

Research shows that, in general, girls make external attributions for success (for example, that the task was easy or they were lucky), while boys make internal attributions for success (for example, their own ability). Many feminists would argue that girls have been brought up with these attitudes being reinforced all around them. From an early age girls learn to perceive that they have less control over their lives than boys – for example, from the story lines in fiction and images in the media. In stories, female characters are still more likely to be portrayed as having things happen to them, while male characters are more often portrayed as being in control and taking the lead (Trowler, 1996).

The influence of school on gender differences
There are many studies that argue that one of the most important factors in explaining the differential achievement of girls and boys is the attitudes and expectations of teachers. Clarricoates (1987) shows the ways in which teachers' expectations of children in primary schools follow gender-stereotyped patterns. Clarricoates found that boys were thought to be more interesting to teach than girls, and that girls were expected to conform and be less disruptive than boys. Because they were perceived to be more demanding, Clarricoates observed that teachers had to spend more time talking to, and interacting with, boys. Also, Clarricoates noted that teachers would gear classroom work towards boys' interests as a means of controlling them.

Although many teachers today do practise anti-sexist education, there is still evidence to suggest that many still stereotype using gender as the criteria for doing so. An HMI report in 1990 cited by Trowler (1996) reports a teacher saying to a class in a biology lesson that involved dissection, 'Now which of you boys will do the cutting?' and 'Girls, let me know if you feel sick' (1996, p. 187). Mac An Ghaill (1994) observed teachers setting boys against girls in order to get tasks completed more quickly; he also noted that the harassment of girls by boys was not taken seriously by male teachers in the school in which he carried out his research.

The curriculum itself is still seen to favour boys. Early research by Lobban (1974) suggested that primary school reading material was stereotyped – in other words, boys were portrayed as heroes in active roles, and girls in the same text books were more often portrayed in domestic situations. Although this study is dated, more recent studies (such as Best, 1993) show that there are still twice as many male characters in pre-school children's books. Female characters are still portrayed in domestic roles (75 per cent), whereas 81 per cent of male characters are portrayed in roles outside the home. Bradshaw *et al* (1995) have shown that although computer software now often represents characters as neither feminine nor masculine, children in their study more often attributed a male identity to the characters than a female one.

Student choice of areas of study often reflects stereotypical views of 'masculine' and 'feminine' subjects. The introduction of the National Curriculum in 1988 undermined some of the old notions of gender-stereotyped subjects in secondary school, as everyone has to follow the same curriculum. However, at A level and in Higher Education, many subjects are still perceived as 'gendered'; social science and languages, for example, are still dominated by female students, while science subjects, maths and computing are largely dominated by male students. It appears, then, that as soon as students are able to choose which subjects to study, gender stereotyping establishes itself. Vocational qualifications after the age of sixteen are also gender stereotyped, with girls choosing courses in hairdressing, beauty therapy and caring services, while boys choose engineering, construction and science-based qualifications (Pilcher, 1999).

It is also important to understand the pressure of the peer group and the need for students to conform. Obviously the influence of teachers is very

important, but the influence of peers within the school environment is also very influential. Children often censure each other if they do not behave in gender typical ways (Walkerdine, 1990). Children often segregate themselves according to gender, and play in groups of girls and boys separated from each other in the playground. Delmont (1990) argues that boys and girls often actively compete against each other in both the classroom and the playground, and consciously set themselves apart as separate groups.

This recent research gives an example of the contradictory nature of the evidence, that in spite of both the home and school environment being disadvantageous to girls, they are in fact doing better than boys in some areas of the curriculum. As we have already noted, girls have always thrived (at least academically) when compared to boys, in the primary school environment. The current trend, however, is that girls are performing better than boys in the secondary school and A level environment. Some researchers, though, would argue that although this is an overall improvement in the performance of girls, it still only represents a partial change. Girls are now performing as well as boys in some subjects, and slightly better in others. Stereotyping of subject choice is still a problem, and the difference in the performance of male and female students is marginal. For example, girls are more likely to take and pass A levels than boys, but boys obtain higher grades overall (Pilcher, 1999). It could therefore be argued that the concern over what is often labelled the current underachievement of boys is a 'moral panic'.

Ethnicity

It is perhaps most important to understand the way in which ethnicity is seen as a factor causing underachievement in society, in the context of racism. This is possibly the most critical factor that underpins the achievement of certain groups. There are two forms of racism that have been the focus of attention in educational research – individual racism and institutional racism. Institutional racism is the one we will focus on in the context of the school environment, but as with the section on gender there are also biological and cultural factors that will be considered as explanations for differential attainment.

The influence of innate ability on educational attainment

In America, Jensen and Eysenk, as late as the 1970s, were still subscribing to the view that black people had lower innate intelligence (measured using IQ tests) than the white population. They suggested that statistical evidence showed that black people scored 10 to 15 points lower on IQ tests than white people.

Commentary

These views have been widely discredited by taking into account environmental factors – particularly the prejudice and discrimination suffered by black people in America over a long period of time. It is impossible to control all the confounding variables that might affect IQ scores in tests as unreliable as these.

The influence of racism in society

There is a history to racism in our own society that cannot be ignored as a factor that has shaped the experience of people from ethnic minorities within the education system. One of the places to start looking at contemporary racism in this society is in the post-war period of immigration in the 1940s and 1950s. By the late 1950s there was a growing resistance to this immigration among some members of the white population; and in 1958 a series of riots, sparked by attacks on people from ethnic minorities, caused policy makers to look to schools to change attitudes.

Prior to this it was assumed that black children would assimilate into British society by accepting and learning British values and traditions. In the mid-1960s, however, Roy Jenkins, the (then) Home Secretary, made a speech that was seen to influence this assimilationist policy towards a more integrationist phase. The outcome of this was the development of multicultural education (Kirby *et al*, 1997).

Multicultural education worked on the assumption that the curriculum might be perceived as Eurocentric. Multicultural education was supposed to combat the underachievement of people from ethnic minorities by making the curriculum reflect the experiences and cultures of all children, not just the white population. The problem, however, was that it was seen by many as condescending and had little impact on the real issue of achievement.

Commentary

- Some theorists actually blame multicultural education for the underachievement of black students.

Stone (1981) argued that meeting the needs of black students through multicultural education was interpreted by teachers as encouraging their abilities in areas such as music and sport. Multicultural education was seen as 'focusing on lifestyle rather than life chances' (Kirby *et al* 1997, p. 298).

- Multicultural education was also seen as ignoring the wider problems of institutional racism in society.
- One of the responses to the problems with multicultural education was for schools to develop more rounded equal opportunities policies that addressed other discrimination that some students might face, such as that on the grounds of gender, sexual orientation, class, disability and so on.
- Right-wing critics of multicultural education argue that assimilationist educational policies are still more appropriate.

Cultural factors explaining ethnic differences in educational attainment

Before the influence of the system itself is examined in more detail, it is interesting to consider research from America that is concerned with the use of verbal and non-verbal communication, and cultural factors that may create problems within the education system in terms of communication between teachers and their students. Bennett (1990) identifies five aspects of ethnicity that are potential sources of student-teacher misunderstanding.

1 **Verbal communication:** Bennett argues that problems with verbal communication can occur for children for whom English is a second language. Many children from ethnic minority backgrounds are thought of as less intelligent by their teachers than their white peers, simply because they do not communicate in 'standard' English (see also the discussion of language codes, page 63).

2 **Non-verbal communication:** Bennett argues that some forms of communication, such as eye contact, are used in different ways by different cultures, and that these signals can be misinterpreted. In some Native American and Asian cultures it is not appropriate to hold eye contact with someone in authority – looking down or away might be misconstrued as disinterest or ignorance by a teacher who did not understand this.

3 **Time orientation:** Mainstream American culture is very time orientated. Time is highly valued and the education system is geared towards appropriate time management. Groups in the population,

such as Hispanic Americans and Native Americans, whose cultures do not stress this sense of urgency are disadvantaged in an education system that does.

4 **Competition and individualism:** Many classroom activities and the system of examinations in schools reward competitive and individualistic behaviour. Bennett argues that Mexican Americans, for example, are more likely to be taught co-operative values at home, which do not fit in with the ethos of their education.

5 **Types of knowledge and learning:** Bennett found that different ethnic groups within the American population prefer different learning styles, depending on their own cultural influences. For example, some prefer listening to tapes of information as well as looking at a book, whereas others learn better without the use of a tape. Some children, whose culture reflects co-operation, prefer to work with others in group work engaged in discovery learning, whereas other prefer an approach based on reception learning (see Chapter 2, pages 31–33).

Many other studies, both British and American, suggest that there are problems with the individual or within the family or the particular communities where children are underachieving. These explanations lay the blame at the door of the underachiever. Although some of the more recent American research has been described here, there are many other rather dated studies that look at the structure of families, linguistic deprivation, low self-esteem and so on as explanations of the underachievement of Afro-Caribbean boys in particular (Trowler, 1996). However, more contemporary studies in Britain are now focusing on racism within the education system itself that accounts for the underachievement of some students, and more positively, the achievement of others. There is, for example, an increasing amount of evidence that suggests that black girls are doing better in exams than their peers (Mirza, 1992), unlike black boys, who are still over-represented among those failing within the education system (Gillborn and Gipps, 1996). What is interesting about the success of these girls is that they do not perceive themselves as conforming but, rather, they see their success as a reaction to racism and a way of overcoming it.

Racism in the education system
Gilroy (1990) argues that the education system sees ethnicity as a white and black issue, and ignores other ethnic groups. He sees this as what he calls essentialist (defining something on the basis of a set of essential characteristics) and reductionist (reducing the problem to one single cause). Gilroy talks about the 'cultural politics of difference', and others like him argue that there are many different forms of identity that need to be considered – including, for example, class, religion and gender.

Much of the research into racism and issues surrounding the status of ethnic minority groups within the education system is inevitably qualitative. Studies are often carried out using observational techniques and interviews (see Key Study 8, below).

KEY STUDY 8

Researcher:	Wright (1992)
Aim:	To investigate the nature of racism in 'multiracial' primary schools.
Method:	Wright studied four multiracial inner-city primary schools in a classroom observation of 970 students and 57 staff, and informal interviews of teachers, support staff and the parents of children. Wright also looked at the test results of three of the four schools.
Results:	In spite of the commitment of the staff to equality of educational opportunity, Wright found considerable discrimination in the classroom. In all the classes, Asian girls were 'invisible' to their teachers, who stereotyped them in terms of their expectations of the girls' traditions and customs. Wright found that the isolation felt by these girls was exacerbated by other children, who picked up on the attitudes of the teachers. Wright also found that teachers' expectations of Afro-Caribbean children were also stereotyped, but in different ways. Wright found that teachers expected Afro-Caribbean boys in particular to be disruptive, and punished them more harshly than white boys exhibiting the same behaviour.
Conclusions:	Wright argues that young children will be affected by their early

---

experiences of racism within the school environment. Not only did children suffer from the racism of their teachers and fellow classmates, but also, when topics relating to ethnic minority concerns were raised by the teachers (looking at religious festivals, for example), the teachers often mispronounced words or names, embarrassing black children and causing white children to laugh. Wright argues that, unintentionally, the teacher helps to make this knowledge seem exotic, unimportant and difficult.

Research, and the broader implications of racism

Many other studies also show that teachers hold stereotypical views of black students. Figueroa (1991) shows how this affects the educational opportunities and experiences of black students in the following ways.

- Through inappropriate assessment – using assessment tools that are culturally biased.
- Through misplacement – by being put in lower streams than test results suggest, on the basis of teacher expectations.
- Through channelling – for example, the over-representation of Afro-Caribbean students in sport rather than mainstream academic subjects.

Although many studies have been outlined here that show the reasons why children from some ethnic minorities are disadvantaged within the system, more recent research focuses on the broader implications of racism and students' experience of it. Some feminist researchers (such as Mirza) are interested in 'de-constructing the myth of black educational underachievement'. Mirza (cited in Kirby *et al*, 1997) argues that there is actually a movement away from the underachievement of ethnic minority children (particularly girls). Statistics show that in post-sixteen education, 56 per cent of students from ethnic minority backgrounds stay in the education system, compared to 37 per cent of white students. In new universities, black students, and particularly female students, are over-represented in relation to their respective population sizes. In new universities, people of Caribbean origin were over-repre-

sented by 43 per cent, Asians by 162 per cent and Africans by 223 per cent. For Mirza it is possible that ' . . . doing well can become a radical strategy. An act of social transformation' (1997, p. 263).

Real Life Application 11: Anti-racist education

Material A: Black sociologist attacks race 'doom and gloom'

At the Association of Teachers of Social Science conference in 1996, Heidi Mirza, then head of Sociology at South Bank University, attacked a government report that recommended the introduction of anti-racist and multicultural educational policies. She argued that multicultural education initiatives detract from the real issues of finding good jobs and structured careers. There are gender differences in educational attainment between black male and female students, and Mirza put many of these down to the opportunities available to black women in the labour market. Black women can use traditionally female jobs such as nursing, that are secure and offer educational opportunities. For black men there are fewer opportunities. Mirza argued that people are quite rational; if there is nothing for them, they will recognize this and are not going to invest in their education. In spite of this, Mirza cited evidence that suggests there are relatively more black men in full-time education than white men (36 per cent compared to 31 per cent). Mirza stated that comparisons are always drawn between black girls and black boys, when more meaningful comparisons should be drawn between black girls and working-class white girls. If these comparisons are made then it is evident that black girls do better. Mirza said: 'I live among black people and education is all anyone talks about. I see so much personal investment.'

Material B: 'Anti-racism doesn't work'

At an equal opportunities conference held by the National Union of Teachers on 6 November 1999, Rosemary Campbell, the black head teacher of Northicote Secondary School in Wolverhampton, said that anti-racist teaching was serving no useful purpose. She told the conference: 'People have learned the terminology. They have learned how to cover their racism and their hatred, but they are still within our profession and doing damage to our people.' Campbell argued that the fundamental basic human rights of all children were paramount and that if these are embraced by the teachers in a school, then racism cannot flourish. Rather than dealing with racial harassment specifically, she prefers to tackle all forms of harassment in the same way. This prevents arguments about whether a specific incident is racist and puts the onus on teachers to deal with every form of harassment they come across. According to Campbell, all that is required in order to create an environment in which all students feel understood and nurtured is basic humanity. She said: 'Too many of us do not have that humanity and our racism rises to the fore. And it is so sad and degrading to see that when it is actually exercised against children.'

Summary

- Heidi Mirza argues that the key issue relating to educational achievement is the opportunities people can look forward to when they achieve their qualifications; it is this that leads to the underachievement of black children rather than lack of motivation or racist practices in the classroom.

- Rosemary Campbell argues that anti-racist education provides a shield for racists to hide behind, and that schools should concentrate on treating all children with respect.

Questions

1 Do you agree that schools should not distinguish between racial harassment and 'ordinary' bullying?

2 Do you feel that students in British schools are generally treated with respect?

3 What type of anti-racist policies does your school or college have?

Class

One of the factors not considered so far in relation to ethnicity is the impact of social class. The text that follows considers it as a factor that shapes educational performance and will include an analysis of ethnicity in relation to class.

As with gender and ethnicity, social class has been examined by many theorists as an explanation for differential educational achievement. Statistics relating to achievement show that the higher the social class, the higher the level of educational achievement.

Innate ability and social class

Some studies show that there is a correlation between measured intelligence and achievement in education. The 1944 Education Act in Britain established the tripartite system of education. This system was based on an IQ test called the 11+. This test was taken in the year before secondary school and was supposed to determine the type of secondary education that was best suited to each individual on the basis of their IQ score. There were three types of school: grammar schools for students with higher measured intelligence, secondary modern schools for students with lower levels of measured intelligence, and a few technical colleges, established in some parts of the country for students for whom a vocational education was considered most appropriate.

Educational psychologists were very influential in helping to develop and establish the system. Once the system was in place it became obvious that there was a correlation between IQ scores and social class, as the overwhelming majority of grammar school children were middle class. This would suggest that there is a link between class and innate intelligence. However, there are many criticisms of the 11+ exam, and the system was eventually largely abandoned in favour of the comprehensive system in which all children, regardless of their ability or social background, go to the same local school.

Commentary

Research into the type of test being used in the 11+ exam shows that it was very culturally biased in favour of the middle class. The types of question were written by middle-class psychologists with the cultural knowledge of middle-class children in mind, and were standardized on middle-class children in a narrow range of schools. For example, many 11+ questions were anagrams of culturally specific knowledge – famous composers, or artists. Some of these questions therefore reflected the cultural capital of the middle classes rather than the working classes. The tests have since been discredited, as most educational psychologists recognize that there can be no such thing as a culture-fair test (see text on assessment in Chapter 2, pages 33–37).

Language and social class

Studies in the 1960s and 70s suggested that language deprivation was a problem for working-class children within the education system. Working-class children were not thought to be using the type of language that was expected in school. One of the most famous studies of this type was carried out by Bernstein (1960). He described the way in which the middle class and working class use different speech codes. Bernstein referred to these as elaborated and restricted speech codes.

Bernstein argued that the characteristics of the restricted code spoken by the working class were:

- short, unfinished sentences
- repetitiveness
- use of question tags ('didn't I?' and so on)
- narrow vocabulary
- bound to a particular social context (since the language is limited to explaining particular situations).

The characteristics of the elaborated code, spoken by the middle class were:

- explicit and detailed sentences
- meaning explained clearly
- use of universalistic language (not tied to a particular context).

Bernstein used the example of working-class and middle-class children being given a series of pictures to describe. He argued that because of the restricted code they were using the working-class children's explanation could only be understood with reference to the pictures, whereas the middle-class children could be understood without reference to the pictures. Bernstein argued that the education system demands and teaches the elaborated code, therefore working-class children are at a disadvantage, and that using a restricted code limited the opportunities for working-class children to acquire some of the skills they needed within the education system.

Commentary

Critics of Bernstein, and others who support his views, argue that the research encourages people to make value judgements about types of speech codes or regional variation in speech patterns for example. They argue that it is more important to understand the difference between language styles rather than looking at one as superior to another.

An example of this approach is adopted by Tizard and Hughes (1986). They examined the ways in which middle-class and working-class mothers and daughters interacted with each other and came to the conclusion that there were no major differences between the linguistic competence of working-class and middle-class women. They argue that a distinction should be drawn between linguistic competence and style of communication.

Cultural capital

It is important to look at other aspects of family life as well as the use of language in trying to explain the differences in educational attainment between working-class and middle-class children.

Bourdieu (1977) uses the term 'cultural capital' to refer to the educational advantages that some families may have, which are of benefit to their children within the education system. It is made up of the cultural activities and knowledge that is valued within the school system. A quote from Judd and Borrill (1991) gives an example of what this means:

Parents and teachers are preparing to drill seven year olds for the new national reading tests . . . Booksellers and publishers were deluged by inquiries last week after the Department of Education issued a list of 51 books that will be used for the tests. At Blackwell's in Oxford and Heffers in Cambridge, ambitious parents, carrying the government's list, scoured the shelves hoping to ensure top marks for their children (1991; cited in Trowler 1996, p. 153).

The influence of school

Many researchers argue that the most important influence on success or failure of the individual student is the school and exam system, rather than a specific factor to do with the individual or the home environment.

Student–teacher interaction

Many studies focus on the interaction between the teacher and the student as a cause of working-class disadvantage. All this research suggests that teachers stereotype students who do not conform to a certain ideal. This ideal 'good' student works hard, follows school rules, behaves well, wants to, and is capable of, answering teacher's questions and writes in standard English (Trowler, 1996). This student is also likely to follow dress codes and subscribe generally to the ethos of the school – taking part in sport and drama for example. Students who do not do this can very quickly become alienated, and will not identify with the school or what it stands for. According to the research it is students from working-class backgrounds who are more likely to become alienated than middle-class ones.

In America, Rist (1970) carried out research to look at the way in which teachers stereotype children even when they are in kindergarten. Rist found that as early as the eighth day of school, the children had been grouped on three separate tables by their teacher. Table 1 was for 'fast learners'; the other two tables were for less able students. Rist, however, believed that in reality it was not ability, but the degree of conformity that children showed to the teacher's own middle-class values that had made the teacher place the children in groups.

There are many similar studies that look at the expectations middle-class teachers have of their students. Like the studies that focus on stereotyping in groups (see Key Study 4, page 27) some of these also look at the likelihood of middle-class children ending up in the top sets or streams in secondary schools. Again, there is very clear evidence that middle-class and working-class children are not placed in sets according to their ability, but according to their social class, and most of these studies found a strong correlation between streaming and performance.

Real Life Application 12:

Boys' underachievement? Not the real question

Carole Regan's article in *Socialist Teacher* highlights some of the problems with research that suggests that boys are underachieving at GCSE, A level and in GNVQs. She suggests that the government has over-reacted to research that is flawed, and that it is ignoring the real inequality in educational achievement.

Regan cites research carried out at Bristol University, in which the sample was a group of middle-class children on an Assisted Places scheme. This research appears to show that girls are outperforming boys. Regan argues that statistics in general show that girls are doing better than boys; but she questions what these statistics really show.

Regan believes that it is really class that is the most important factor explaining differential achievement. She argues that the small gender gap (nationally about 4 per cent) in those taking GCSEs is nowhere near as severe as the gap between stu-

dents of different social classes. Regan cites statistics for gender that show that around 84 per cent of boys, compared to 88 per cent of girls, take GCSEs. She compares this to statistics for Kingston on Thames (Surrey) and Tower Hamlets (London). In Kingston on Thames, 51 per cent of boys, compared to 64 per cent of girls, achieved grades A–C at GCSE level in 1998, compared to 24 per cent of boys and 28 per cent of girls in Tower Hamlets.

Regan gives examples of government initiatives to combat gender inequality in educational performance, whereas she argues the government is not addressing the more significant problem of class-based inequality.

Article adapted from *Socialist Teacher*, 65, spring 1998

Summary

- There is some evidence that girls outperform boys at school, but gender differences are much smaller than differences between social classes.
- The government should be doing more to tackle class inequality rather than spending so much time and resources on gender inequality.

Questions

1 Based on your own classroom experience, why do you think girls are now achieving at the same level, and sometimes above the level of boys?

2 Do you agree with Regan that class is the most important issue? List the reasons for your answer.

Special educational needs

The text that follows takes a brief look at the history of special education, followed by definitions of, and identification of, learning difficulties, inclusion and segregation of students with special needs, and giftedness.

A history of special education

In the early part of the 20th century, ideas about the provision of education for children with special needs was based on a medical model of 'defects'. This model focused on difference rather than normality, on illness rather than well being, and particularly on the 'problem' with the child (Lewis, 1999). Children were given medically diagnosed categories, with the emphasis on deficit rather than potential. Therefore, it is hardly surprising that education for children with special educational needs originally took the form of separate, special schools for those who were thought to need them. Psychometric testing by early psychologists (such as Cyril Burt) also confirmed this type of approach to disability and difference.

The education reforms of 1944

In 1944, significant reforms to the education system were brought into effect. Most of these reforms were directed at mainstream education and the provision of free education for all. The 1944 Act also addressed certain aspects of education for children with special needs. However, its approach to, and definitions of, children with special needs was not as liberating as its prescriptions for education in general. The Act still focused on a medical model of disability. It established eleven categories of 'handicap', and children falling into these categories were described in terms of the 'treatment' they could receive. Special schools were still seen as the most appropriate way to educate children with special needs, although limited recognition was given to the provision of education in mainstream schools. The 1944 Act still referred to children who 'suffered from a disability of mind or body', and so clearly focused on 'special schools' as catering for 'handicapped' children.

Education throughout the 1960s and 70s

In the 1960s and 70s, work with children with special needs moved towards an approach favoured by behaviourist psychologists. This approach stressed the need to use operant conditioning techniques. Behaviourists rejected the medical model and advocated an approach that dealt with only what they could observe. This was criticized as a major weakness by some. However, this work was very important because it stressed the possibility of modifying the problems of children with special needs and placed the responsibility of that modification with the teacher (Lewis, 1999).

Behaviourist techniques were seen as very effective in helping with particular difficulties – self-help skills, for example. But they were seen to be less effective in helping children with tasks that involved more understanding. As Lewis argues:

Neo-behaviourists attempted to meet some of the criti-

cisms of behaviourists' approaches by giving some place to 'cognitive mediation'. This attempted to explain how, for example, memory of failure might inhibit a child from reading words correctly despite being consistently praised when they were read correctly. It was recognized that children were responding not to some neutral event in teaching but to their perceptions of that event. So for an adolescent with learning difficulties, receiving praise from the teacher for correct answers might be perceived as embarrassing rather than encouraging. Thus positive reinforcement might be counter-productive' (Lewis 1999, p. 47).

The 1960s and 70s paved the way for a new approach to special needs. Attitudes to special education in general started to change, and in part the behaviourist initiatives made the teaching of children with learning difficulties seem more accessible to teachers in mainstream schools. These ideas helped to promote the possibility of inclusion of children with special educational needs.

The Warnock Report

The Warnock Report in 1978 was based on the findings of a committee set up to review the provision for children with mental and physical disabilities. The report made 225 recommendations, one of which was to abolish the use of categories, which it saw as damaging and irrelevant. The Warnock Committee advocated a **continuum** of special needs, rather than discrete categories. The Committee's research suggested that only 2 per cent of the school population required separate educational provision, but that there were another 18 per cent of children who would require special provision in normal schools. Warnock argued that this 18 per cent had always been there, but that there had not been a consistent effort to integrate these children in the system.

However, legislation is gradually catching up with these recommendations. The Warnock Report formed the basis of the 1981 Education Act's policies (enforced in 1983) on special educational needs (SEN), which introduced a quite different approach to the definition of children with SEN:

A child will have a special educational need if s/he has a learning difficulty requiring special educational provision. The 'learning difficulty' includes not only physical and mental disabilities, but also any kind of learning difficulty experienced by a child, provided that it is significantly greater than that of the majority of children of the same age.

The Act went further in stating that the education of children with SEN should be carried out in ordinary schools where possible. The Act therefore emphasized an approach that is in favour of inclusion and integration, rather than separation and isolation. This approach advocates that children with special needs should be treated as individuals, and that the particular resources that each child needs should be allocated to that child – for example, that the child should have a learning support teacher with them in the classroom, rather than being taken out of the class.

Recent educational reform

More recent educational reform (such as the Education Act of 1993) has continued to push for an inclusive approach. There are now legal requirements that oblige schools to provide for children with learning difficulties (in line with a Code of Practice established in 1994). All schools had to publish their SEN policies before August 1995, and name a SEN Co-ordinator (SENCO) on their staff (Child, 1997). The 1994 Code of Practice is currently under review and a new Code is due to be published in 2001. Similarly, sixth form colleges and colleges of further education have to appoint an inclusive learning co-ordinator, and find ways of improving education and training for those with learning difficulties and/or disabilities, and of widening participation among people under-represented in further education (FEFC, 1998).

Commentary

The medical model is now criticized for being dehumanizing, and treating children like objects (Lewis, 1999). It groups vague symptoms together and assumes they can be treated in the same way. Some, however, draw attention to the value of some parts of this model. For example, Bailey (1998) argues that this kind of model includes the rigorous approach of a scientific analysis to the problems, in order to establish causes and treatments.

Definitions of learning difficulties

In its broadest sense, the term 'special needs' can be applied to any student who requires some sort of special educational treatment as a result of difficulties in one or more of the following areas.

- **Social–emotional:** students with ADHD, autism and so on.
- **Physical:** students with sensory deficits (visual or

hearing impairments), cerebral palsy, epilepsy and so on.
- **Intellectual:** students with **learning difficulties**.

Social–emotional and physical difficulties can have a lasting impact on an individual's education, but these kinds of problem tend to be diagnosed and treated by professionals working outside the educational system (for example, clinical psychologists), although specialist educational units do exist for children with such difficulties.

The term 'learning difficulty' is used to define a number of conditions. Most descriptions of learning difficulties highlight four groups of characteristics (LeFrançois, 1997).

1 There is a noticeable difference between expected behaviour and actual behaviour, in terms of performance in tests and so on.
2 There is an uneven pattern of academic achievement that cannot be explained by other factors (such as disinterest).
3 Learning disabilities are often noticed in the use of written or spoken language or numeracy.
4 Problems associated with learning disabilities do not result from other problems, such as impaired hearing or vision.

Historically, the various terms used to describe different degrees of learning difficulty (**mild, moderate, severe** and **profound**) were related to specific IQ levels. This approach tended to label individuals, and to ignore their actual abilities and difficulties. More recently, there is a recognition that all students can have difficulties with their learning, but that certain students have difficulties that require special help. Students with learning difficulties are generally categorized as follows.

- **Moderate learning difficulty (MLD):** students who can be taught in mainstream schools with some learning support.
- **Severe learning difficulty (SLD):** students who require a much higher degree of specialist support – usually within special units or schools.
- **Profound and multiple learning difficulty (PMLD):** students with very serious intellectual difficulties, combined with sensory and other physical impairments.

There is also a category for students with difficulties that are not related to general impairments in intellectual ability.

- **Specific learning difficulty (SPLD):** these refer to conditions such as **dyslexia** and **dyscalcula**.

Identifying learning difficulties

The 1994 Code of Practice (see page 66) describes five stages through which school children will pass if they are suspected of having a learning difficulty.

- **Stage 1**: if teachers feel that a certain child may have SEN, they place the child on the school's **SEN Register**, and try to help the child as best they can within the classroom. In some cases, initial recognition of a potential learning difficulty may come from a parent.

- **Stage 2**: if the individual teachers feel they are failing to provide the support and help needed by the a child, they refer him/her to the SEN Co-ordinator (SENCO), who takes responsibility for the child's special educational needs. The SENCO draws up an **Individual Education Plan** (IEP) to monitor the level of difficulty experienced by the child and to see if the school's interventions are helping.

- **Stage 3**: if the SENCO feels that the child is not being helped enough, s/he will use specialist support from outside the school (educational psychologist, speech and language therapy, family consultation centres, hearing advisory service, visual impairment advisory service and so on). These outside agencies contribute to the IEP.

- **Stage 4**: if, following two reviews of the IEP, it is still felt that the child is not making appropriate progress, the school applies to the LEA for statutory assessment of the child, in order to obtain extra resources and help.

- **Stage 5**: if the child receives an SEN statement from the local education authority (LEA), then there are mandatory requirements, and extra funding, for the school to provide special help for the child (for example, annual review of needs and learning support assistants in the classroom).

Commentary

- An SEN statement is a formal recognition that a child has a special need as a result of some kind of learning difficulty. It is useful to the child to be statemented in this way as it means that the child will receive extra support; without a statement, the LEA will not provide any funds. In practice, the special help received by statemented children often consists of a learning support assistant (LSA). The LSA is an adult who spends a specified number of hours a week in the classroom with the statemented child. However, it is not always the case that this is the most effective way of supporting a particular child.

- In marginal cases of learning difficulty, it can be quite hard to get a child statemented, and parents often have a long fight to achieve this. As a result, parents who have the resources for this (for example, they are middle-class with a high level of cultural capital) are more likely to get their children statemented and therefore more likely to obtain special educational provision.

Diagnostic tests

There are various diagnostic tests that are used with children who are suspected of having a learning disability. RLA 13 (see below) looks at some recent research into the diagnosis of dyslexia that could revolutionize the way in which dyslexia is identified.

Real Life Application 13:

Research puts dyslexia test on new footing

A simple new test has been designed to screen for dyslexia. It has been developed by Kathleen Kelly, a teacher at a special school in Oldham, and involves children counting while standing on one leg.

The British Dyslexia Association estimates that between 6 per cent and 10 per cent of the school population have dyslexia which, left undiagnosed, can cause severe frustration and anxiety. Kelly's test can differentiate between children who have dyslexia and those who may be suspected of having dyslexia, but in fact have difficulties associated with learning English as an additional language. Her research is based on previous evidence that shows that dyslexic children may have problems with 'automatic' tasks, such as balancing. In a trial involving 210 eleven-year-old children, the test was 98 per cent accurate in diagnosing dyslexia, as opposed to difficulties with English.

The test takes about ten minutes and can be used on children who are eight years and over. It involves testing a child's 'wobble factor' under timed conditions, then comparing this to a second balancing test in which an individualized counting task is also included. The counting is to distract the child from the effort of balancing. The results of the test are then followed up as it cannot recognize the severity of the condition.

Article by Karen Thornton adapted from the *Times Educational Supplement*, 25 June 1999

Summary

- Kathleen Kelly has developed a new test for diagnosing dyslexia based on children's ability to balance.

Questions

1 Why is it so important to identify children with dyslexia?

2 Describe the advantages and disadvantages of Kathleen Kelly's test for dyslexia.

Dyslexia and non-native English speakers

The application described in RLA 13 is interesting and very relevant in the light of other evidence, which suggests that children whose first language is not English are not being diagnosed with dyslexia. In an article in the *Times Higher Education Supplement* (11 June 1999), Karen Thornton cites the opinions of Lindsay Peer, Education Director of the British Dyslexia Association. Peer argues that many children who are trying to learn English, and who are also dyslexic are not being diagnosed because their problems are put down to their difficulty with English. These children are missing out on vital support, as they may also be having difficulty with their first language as a result of their dyslexia. Thornton notes that the Department for Education and Employment is funding a review of research into dyslexia and multilingualism.

Inclusion or segregation

Whether to include or segregate children with SEN into mainstream schools is still a contentious issue, and one that is not easily resolved. There is certainly a trend towards inclusion both within this country and internationally at the present time. Many theorists believe that inclusive education for children with SEN should be thought of as a 'right', whereas others believe that it may mean that the teaching of SEN children becomes less effective.

Continuum of provision

Public policy in Britain supports the inclusion of as many SEN children as possible in mainstream schools. The recent Green Paper on SEN (DfEE, 1997) states that there should be a continuum of provision, including special schools where they are needed (Hornby, 1999). The Green Paper states that:

We support the UNESCO Salemanca World Statement on Special Needs Education. This calls on governments to adopt the principle of inclusive education, enrolling all children in regular schools unless there are compelling reasons for doing otherwise (cited in Hornby, 1999, p. 52).

A recent American study of 1,000 school districts (Lipsky and Gartner, 1998; cited by Hornby, 1999) showed that there were seven important factors that were necessary to make inclusion a success.

1 Visionary leadership
2 Collaboration
3 Use of careful assessment
4 Support for staff and students
5 Appropriate funding
6 Parental involvement
7 Effective models to adapt the curriculum and teaching practices in appropriate ways.

Initiatives and criticisms of inclusion

The kinds of initiative that are likely to work are obviously very costly. In Britain there are different schools of thought about the best way to include children with SEN. Some theorists would argue that total inclusion is important, whereas others, such as Marston (1996) found that students who were taken out of classes and taught in special groups for some activities did better than those who received support in classes.

One of the criticisms of full inclusion is that it focuses on the process of the education rather than the outcome, and on the curriculum of mainstream education rather than the curriculum of SEN (Hornby, 1999).

Some studies have focused on the attitudes of SEN children and their parents to inclusive education. The majority of parents supported inclusion if there were sufficient resources provided alongside the programme. Kidd and Hornby (1993) carried out a survey in which they questioned 29 sets of parents of children who had 'moderate' learning difficulties. These children had been transferred from special schools into mainstream schools. Kidd and Hornby found that 65 per cent of the parents and 76 per cent of the children were 'satisfied' with the transfer. However, they found that there was a difference in how happy the parents were depending on what kind of inclusion the children experienced. Some 47 per cent of parents of children included in mainstream classes were happy, compared to 92 per cent of parents of children placed in units in mainstream schools (Hornby, 1999).

As early as 1978, Warnock distinguished between **social** integration (integration in leisure time), **locational** integration (where a separate unit is located on a mainstream school site) and **functional** integration (where children are included in mainstream schools) (Child, 1997). The trend towards inclusion is growing, but there is still a 'substantial proportion' of children in segregated units, and there is still some way to go before there is enough evidence about the outcomes of inclusion to draw valid conclusions.

Commentary

Although inclusion is seen as a very positive strategy by some educationalists, it is considered idealistic and impractical by others.

- Some critics have argued that social and academic inclusion happens at the expense of good and appropriate education for the other children in the class; in other words, if a student with special needs is taught within a mainstream class, s/he might need extra attention from the teacher, or may be disruptive or difficult in the class, and this could harm other children's education. On the other hand, it can be argued that the other children in the class benefit a great deal from working with students with special needs and that inclusive education helps to remove stereotypes and ignorance (see RLA 14, next column).

- It is also argued that children with SEN are themselves better off in segregated classrooms as this enables them to gain social support from others with similar difficulties, and it allows LEAs to concentrate its specialist teachers and resources in one place. The objection to this is that the disadvantage of keeping children with certain difficulties together is that it makes it harder for them to integrate fully into society once they leave school. If specific teacher skills are required to deal with certain children, then it is easier (and cheaper) to train a few teachers and concentrate them in specialist units, but this is not necessarily better in educational terms; the attitudes and skills of teachers are fundamentally important, and there is a need to combat negative attitudes from inexperienced and untrained staff.

- At first glance it may seem that providing special schools and units for children with SEN is a more expensive option than integrating those children into mainstream classrooms. However, the cost of providing specialist resources and proper training for teachers in all schools is much more costly than concentrating on fewer teachers in special units. One criticism that has been made of recent practice is that children with SEN have been integrated into mainstream classrooms 'on the cheap', and that the training and special resources have not been provided to an appropriate level.

Real Life Application 14:

Inclusive education is a 'human right'

A human rights approach to inclusive education argues that the problems of inclusion do not come from the individual, but the discriminatory attitudes in society. The article argues that:

Issues of social justice, equity and choice are central to the demands for inclusive education . . . Special education entails a discourse of exclusion and this is seen as a particularly offensive aspect of provision.

From this perspective, no one should be left out of school. The article argues that special schools exist because of the limitations of mainstream schools. The article criticizes the government Green Paper (see page 68) because it argues that it does not make explicit where the funding will come from for the resources needed in inclusive education. The article concludes with a plea for inclusive education:

Inclusive education is about belonging. It is about citizenship with all the entitlements and responsibilities involved. It is about the enrichment of all children and the importance of establishing a sense of community based on co-operation, respect and the celebration of difference with dignity.

Adapted from an article (which reproduced extracts from a lecture given by Len Barton, Professor of Education at Sheffield University), in *Socialist Teacher*, no. 65, 1998

Summary

- Len Barton argues that the argument between inclusion and segregation should not just be about practical issues; inclusive education is a human right.

Giftedness

The final section of text in this chapter explores the definitions of giftedness, how to identify giftedness, educating gifted children and the problems such children might have.

Definitions of giftedness

There is no single agreed definition of giftedness. What defines giftedness is, to an extent, described by what measure is used by the psychologist or teacher (Child, 1997). A parent may suspect that their child is especially talented in a particular area, or seems very able compared to his or her peers, but it is likely to be a teacher who realizes that a child is gifted. A number of different ability tests are used because there are a number of factors that are characteristic of giftedness, as listed below.

- Inherited ability
- Personal attributes
- The environment and learning experiences of the individual child
- The individual child's talent.

An HMI report (1992; cited in Child, 1997) on the education of gifted children states:

The majority of educationalists working in this field accept criteria which include general intellectual ability, specific aptitude in one or more subjects, creative or productive thinking, leadership qualities, ability in creative or performing arts and psychomotor ability. The term 'very able' is intended to refer broadly to the top 5 per cent of the ability range in any of these areas, while the term 'exceptionally able' refers to that tiny minority . . . functioning several years beyond their age group.

Identifying giftedness

The main way of recognizing giftedness has been to measure the performance of gifted children in relation to **norm referenced** measures of ability (for an explanation of norm referencing see Chapter 2, pages 35–36). One of the problems with the process of testing potentially gifted students is that the types of tests available may not be able to test their abilities adequately. Some education authorities use **checklists** that list the main characteristics of gifted children (Child, 1997).

Many researchers look at the performance of children in school and may take account of the perceptions of parents. One such study is described in Key Study 9 (see below)

KEY STUDY 9

Researcher: Freeman (1979)

Aim: Freeman looked at the relationship between high IQ and the environment in which the child grows up and is educated.

Method: Freeman used three groups of 70 children: the **target sample** was children whose parents had joined the National Association for Gifted Children (NAGC). The **matched control** sample was made up of children in the same classes as the original sample, who got the same score on the Raven's Progressive Matrices test (a **culture-fair** measure of intellectual aptitude). The **random control sample** consisted of other children chosen at random from the school. The children in the target and matched control samples were assessed using the Raven's test. All the children selected were then tested using intelligence, personality, creativity and music ability tests. The children and their parents were all interviewed.

Results: The matched control group who scored the same on the Raven's test as the target group, scored lower on the general ability tests. Mothers of the target children tended to have reached higher-level occupations and put greater pressure on their children than the control groups; they complained more about their children's schooling. However, Freeman found no differences between the groups on physical and emotional

---

development or personality profiles.

Conclusions: Freeman concluded that children with parents who considered them to be gifted would score more highly on general ability tests, but not on the culture-fair Raven's test. Therefore, using only general IQ measures to identify gifted children would miss those from poor educational environments; it is important to use a measure that identifies all gifted children, regardless of social background (for an example of such a measure see RLA 16, page 73).

General traits of giftedness

Using general traits that seem to recur in many of the studies of gifted children, their personal qualities include high intelligence, good memory, acute creative thinking abilities, and early development in talking, reading, writing, perseverance and concentration (Child, 1997).

A study by Shore and Kanevsky (1993) showed that there are seven particular traits of a gifted learner.

1 An exceptional memory and knowledge base
2 Very good metacognitive abilities
3 A very quick response to test questions
4 Understanding problems very clearly – understanding what is missing and what is irrelevant
5 Awareness of how to use knowledge effectively
6 Flexibility
7 Preference for complexity in problem-solving tasks.

Renzulli, Reis and Smith (1981; cited in LeFrançois, 1997) argue that giftedness can be defined by three characteristics. These are either shown by the student or a teacher would recognize that the student has the potential to achieve them.

1 High ability (high achievement or high IQ)
2 High creativity
3 High commitment.

Both the previous studies and the other definitions that we have looked at so far do appear to recognize that there are some common features of giftedness even if there is no single definition.

Educating gifted children

There are many approaches to educating gifted children, and theorists are divided as to the most effective and appropriate way to do this. The two main ways that will be considered here are **acceleration** and **enrichment**.

Acceleration happens when a student goes through the education system much more quickly than his or her peers, and is able to work at a higher level. There are different ways in which this can happen. For example, a child might enter school early or, more likely, once s/he is in school, miss a year and go into the year above. Gifted children often take exams early, and sometimes, though rarely, children go on to university at a much younger age than normal. The media occasionally report on these exceptional cases. One example in Britain is the case of Ruth Lawrence, whose A levels enabled her to go to St Hughs, Oxford at the age of twelve. She received her BA two years later and her PhD when she was seventeen (Child, 1997).

Enrichment involves giving gifted children a curriculum that is modified to suit their needs. Enrichment means that children are not usually separated from their peers, but that they are given exercises and resources to help them to reach their potential. They may be separated for some lessons or they might simply have access to materials that they can use that are different to those provided for other children. Renzulli *et al* (1981) developed an enrichment model that they called the **revolving door model**. They target children whose achievements are in the top 25 per cent of students, and they provide them with enrichment materials. Students can enter or leave these programmes as they want to (hence the name), and they tend to be school-wide rather than very exclusive.

Freeman (1997) criticizes the use of amateur help for children who are gifted; some people have set up voluntary groups and Saturday schools, for example. He argues that it is important to train teachers so that they can provide the level of education that is needed in mainstream schools.

Many of the strategies that are used with gifted children are also beneficial to other students and are examples of good practice in teaching. For instance, using individualized teaching plans is good for all students. It is also important for all students to be measured against their own potential, and not always measured against other students. Using this type of measurement, it does not matter if the students are gifted or not, as they are striving to do better than themselves. There is also the non-academic curriculum to be considered; school is a social as well as an academic place where students learn more than what is in the curriculum. All students, gifted or not, benefit from the social relationships they develop in school and the support and encouragement of their teachers and peers, both within and outside the classroom.

Commentary

- One of the problems with acceleration is the way in which a student is inevitably isolated from his or her peers. There may be serious social and psychological consequences of this isolation.
- Most theorists would acknowledge that there is no clear evidence to suggest that one of the methods is better than the other. In fact, it may be that they are not so different, at least in their approach to education. Some would argue that acceleration programmes are, broadly speaking, very like enrichment programmes.
- Whether a student is on an enrichment or an acceleration programme, one of the most important issues is if they are taught alone or with other children. Rogers (1993) cited in LeFrançois (1997) argues that grouping children who are gifted is more effective than educating them alone.
- In spite of the research that goes on into the concept of giftedness and the provision of education for gifted children, there are many gifted children who are educated in mainstream schools without any formal provision. They may never be recognized as gifted, or the school may attempt to make some provision for them, by providing what are sometimes referred to as individualized educational plans (in other words, some form of enrichment outside a formal context).

Problems for gifted children

Although we have so far considered the recognition and teaching of children who are gifted it is important to remember that these children, rather like children who have learning difficulties, suffer problems in the education system. While these problems may not be unique to this group they are none the less important to consider the effect they can have on learning and performance.

Seifert (1991) lists a number of the problems that gifted children may face. One of these is pressure from their parents. Parents may expect too much of their children, and unintentionally cause their children to feel very stressed. Parents might also criti-

cize the school if they feel that the teacher is focusing on the majority of the children at the expense of their own gifted child. Motivation is also likely to be a problem, as gifted students may become demotivated and bored by a standard curriculum. One of the other difficulties gifted students may face is a lack of friends, even in mainstream education using enrichment, because most other students might not have common interests with their gifted peer. RLA 15 (see below) highlights some of these problems, and what teachers might do about them.

Real Life Application 15:
Scared of becoming a gifted outcast

In his article for the *Times Educational Supplement*, Neil Munro reports on a lecture given by Miraca Gross, Associate Professor of Gifted Education at the University of New South Wales, Australia. In her lecture, Gross talked about 'hostility' from other students that could cause the underachievement of gifted students or, much worse, could cause them to commit suicide. She described the case of a Scottish teenager who committed suicide after she had been attacked by fellow pupils who threatened to cut off her hair if she did well in her Highers.

Gross argued that: 'It is difficult to display or use your gifts or talents if you know you are going to become an outcast.' She said that giftedness was likely to be 'driven underground' because pupils do not want to be different or unpopular.

Gross said that gifted children walk, talk and read earlier than their peers. She said that research has shown that while 5 per cent of the general population of children are reading by the time they go to school, 50 per cent of gifted children are doing so.

However, she cited research from Australia which showed that gifted children deliberately stopped reading within two weeks of starting school because of peer pressure, and the parents of gifted children did not tell teachers that their children could read when they started school. She argued that teachers were more willing to accept information about children's difficulties than their strengths.

Gross argued that teachers should make children proud of their achievements. She said, 'Conceit says "I am gifted and I am better than you". Pride says, "I am gifted and I can be better than me".'

She said that teachers should be aware of the range of abilities amongst their students. There is an eight-year span in the reading ages of average students in the first year of secondary school in Scotland, which has huge implications for how they are taught.

Gross also warned about the need to recognize that some children may have what she calls a 'double label': they may be gifted *and* dyslexic for example. These children can be misdiagnosed and teachers often concentrate on their weaknesses rather than their strengths.

Article adapted from the *Times Educational Supplement,* 27 June 1997

Summary

- In her work on giftedness Gross warns against the complacency of teachers when teaching and assessing students. She argues that students can be made to feel isolated and different because of the lack of recognition and encouragement they receive in school, and also because they can be picked on by peers who do not understand their situation.

Questions

1 What are the possible risks for students who are open about their giftedness?

2 What strategies should schools use to help all students feel included whatever their abilities?

Gifted children from ethnic minorities
A separate but related issue is the lack of gifted children identified from ethnic minority backgrounds. This is obviously an important omission, as it is not that children from ethnic minorities are less able, but that there is a problem with the system of identification (see pages 58–62) on cultural differences for a discussion of the achievement of children from ethnic minority backgrounds). Newcomb Belcher and Fletcher-Carter (1999) state that, in America, identification practices

. . . almost inevitably identify children with a background of high socio-economic status and exclude cul-

turally and linguistically different children' (1999, p. 17).

They go on to argue that using norm-referenced, standardized tests to identify giftedness is problematic in culturally diverse populations. RLA 16 (see below) looks at a research project they were involved in that addresses some of these issues.

Real Life Application 16:
Growing gifted students in the desert

Newcomb Belcher and Fletcher-Carter were involved in a three-year community-based project in the south-west United States to look at the development of assessment tools that would help with the identification of potentially gifted students in a community that is 96 per cent Hispanic.

The community-based assessment involved the use of an inventory that listed the potential abilities of students. It was given to the community, parents, students and teachers of the students, so that they could rate the students using a 4 point Likert scale. The inventories were written in Spanish and English.

When Newcomb Belcher and Fletcher-Carter compared the results of standard psychometric assessment tools with the community-based assessment they had helped to devise, they found that the number of students identified as gifted rose from three to 24 as a result.

Adapted from an article in *Teaching Exceptional Children,* 17 Sept/Oct 1999

Summary

- Newcomb Belcher and Fletcher-Carter show quite clearly that standard assessment tools are inadequate for children from ethnic minority families. They show that the characteristics associated with cultural diversity may hide giftedness and thus advocate the use of alternative measurements for children from ethnic minority backgrounds.

Questions

1 What are the advantages of community based assessment compared to standard psychometric testing?

2 Is enough done in the UK to identify and teach gifted children?

Sample essay questions

1 Choosing two of the three factors, discuss the ways in which class, gender and ethnicity can affect educational performance in schools.

2 Compare and contrast inclusion and segregation as ways of teaching children who have special needs.

3 Describe the way in which gifted children can be 'hot-housed' within the education system.

A Advice on answering essay questions

Chapter 1

1   This question is asking you to set out the main points of the behaviourist, humanist and cognitive perspectives, and relate each to educational practice in general terms.

2   Behaviourists carry out controlled experiments, often on animals, in order to demonstrate their theories, whereas humanists tend to rely on personal experience and insight. This essay is asking you to criticize each approach from the point of view of the other.

3   Here, you are being asked to examine the kinds of assumption made by each psychological perspective. For example, where does each perspective stand in the nature–nurture debate? Other issues you could consider are reductionism, free will versus determinism and so on.

4   In this essay, you should describe and evaluate the two different ways of running a classroom (perhaps focusing on a particular sector – say, primary, secondary or post-16).

Chapter 2

1   In order to answer this question you should describe behaviourist theories about motivating students through external reinforcers, and criticize and evaluate these by describing a humanist approach to motivating students. Include the work of Lepper and Green, and Maslow in your essay. You could also evaluate the behaviourist approach by describing the cognitive approach to motivation, which argues that people make conscious decisions about their actions, rather than simply being manipulated by external reinforcers or internal needs. Give some relevant examples to illustrate your answer.

2   In this essay you could look at the work of Gagné, Bruner and Ausubel in order to illustrate a range of approaches to teaching methods. You could also include behaviourist and humanist

approaches to teaching as an evaluation of the cognitive approach.

3   In this essay you should describe a number of diagnostic assessment methods, such as those used to diagnose dyslexia and giftedness. You could also describe a number of formative assessment tools – for example, psychometric tests such as IQ tests. You should consider whether these tests are reliable and valid, and in what ways they are problematic. Evaluate the tests you have described.

Chapter 3

1   These should include behaviour modification, cognitive behaviour therapy and fostering prosocial behaviour. Evaluation points include the effectiveness of these techniques, the practical implications of using them in the classroom and the psychological perspectives on which they are based.

2   This question asks you to make some practical suggestions based on the general techniques described in the first essay. However, the focus of this essay is on preventing 'bad' behaviour before it takes place, rather than attempting to deal with it afterwards.

3   Here, you are required to take into account lay-out of furniture in the room, what goes on the walls and the effects of noise temperature, light and colour to make practical suggestions about classroom design. Your design will depend on the type of teaching or learning that is supposed to be going on in the room, and may take practical issues, such as cost, into account.

Chapter 4

1   In this essay you should describe the ways in which gender, ethnicity and class can influence the attainment of individual students. Pay particular attention to the range of factors that may be an influence, from innate ability to the way students are treated in school. If you look at social

class in your essay, pay particular attention to the influence of social class on either of the other two factors (gender or ethnicity). Make sure you are aware of the recent debates in the *underachievement* and *overachievement of* these groups, and use recent press reports, if you can find any, to illustrate your answer.

2 In this essay you should examine different approaches to teaching children with special needs. Briefly describe the history of SEN in Britain. Consider the needs of children with different types of difficulty, and the range of help and support a mainstream school can give.

3 In this essay you should consider what is meant by 'giftedness', and evaluate the various approaches to teaching gifted children, including acceleration and enrichment.

A Advice on answering short answer questions

Chapter 1

RLA 1

1 This depends on whether the children are able to *transfer* the learning to other situations. This is more likely to happen if the children receive some kind of intrinsic reinforcement for their behaviour, in addition to the extrinsic material and social rewards provided by the tokens.

2 This would require a controlled experiment in which one group of participants was offered tokens and another was given equivalent amounts of attention, but no tokens. Behaviour would have to be carefully measured, before and after the intervention for both groups, and followed up over a long period of time to see if the effects are permanent.

3 Without consistency in providing reinforcement children become confused and are in danger of developing *learned helplessness*, in which they feel they are not able to influence what happens to them by behaving in certain ways; this can make children passive and depressed.

4 Token economies have been criticized for being de-humanising in that they attempt to manipulate other people's behaviour. In this case, the tokens seem to be an excuse for social reinforcement, but some people would argue that the children are still not being offered the freedom to choose how to behave.

RLA 2

1 Discussion point. You should give your personal opinions on whether you agree with Rogers' principles.

2 If Summerhill students wish to apply to Higher Education, or to jobs that require formal qualifications, then they may experience difficulties. On the other hand, if Summerhill is successful in providing its students with other educational benefits, then in many ways they will be better equipped for the 'real world' than students who have experienced more traditional education.

3 Summerhill is a private school, so the students there are from materially well off backgrounds; there may be less pressure on these students to earn a living later in life. The suitability of a particular individual may depend on the child's previous experience of education, their outlook on life and their parents' attitudes towards education. Critics of Summerhill sometimes accuse it of providing education that is only suitable for middle-class people. The kind of humanist approach exemplified at Summerhill was tried out in a small number of state primary schools in the 1970s, but this was met with a very mixed response and the experiments did not last long.

4 The implication here is that many of the problems faced by Summerhill is that it is a humanist island in a culture not particularly sympathetic to its principles. It is possibly true that, as long as colleges, universities and employers continue to demand formal academic qualifications, the Summerhill approach will be restricted to a handful of schools.

RLA 3

1 Should Key Skills be embedded into the mainstream curriculum by being entirely taught and assessed in other lessons, or should they be presented as a stand-alone programme? Maybe, the best solution is a combination of the two approaches. Describe the advantages and disadvantages of each solution to the problem of how to teach Key Skills.

2 Do you think that learning Key Skills would make you a better student or a better person? Would it help you do better in your examination subjects or be useful when you are applying for a job? Consider both of these questions before you give your answer.

3 Is it necessary to take a Key Skills qualification in order to prove that you have attained certain

competencies? Who will take notice of these qualifications? Consider both of these questions before you give your answer.

Chapter 2

RLA 4

1 List your GCSE predictions and your actual grades.

2 Discussion point: Were you motivated to work harder by your teachers' predictions of your exam grades?

3 Colleges and universities could invite applications from students after their A level results are published; the problem with this is that it leaves very little time to sort out admissions before the beginning of the autumn term. This could be solved by changing the timings of university or school terms. Also, instead of using predictions to motivate students or to report on their progress, teachers could focus on actual performance in tests, coursework or modular exams.

RLA 5

1 Examples of formative assessment might be aptitude tests, feedback from essays, tests or end-of-year exams.

2 Formative assessment may be effective because detailed feedback on essays can help focus students on the skills they need to address in order to improve their performance.

Chapter 3

RLA 6

1 Four categories of pupils are described as being at particular risk of exclusion. For each, conclusions can be drawn about why those children are at risk, and this sheds light on the causes of problem behaviour.

2 Suggestions may include disciplinary measures against the perpetrators, counselling for bullies and their victims, and ways of tackling the root causes of bullying in a school.

RLA 7

1 ADHD may be caused by physiological under-arousal, leading the individual to seek environmental stimulation in inappropriate ways. Ritalin causes arousal and therefore reduces the need to behave in symptomatic ways.

2 If children are regularly provided with instant gratification, they may become impatient with any delay. This impatience could lead to frustration and from there to the behaviours associated with ADHD.

3 A behaviourist teacher may try to ignore the child's disruptive or inappropriate behaviour, and reward good behaviour, such as sitting down or concentrating for a while on work (see section on Behaviour Modification, page 44).

RLA 8

1 They focus on students as individuals and pay attention to factors in students' lives that might influence their behaviour; they look at interpersonal skills and they are democratic.

2 The research was not an unqualified success; Moreno and Torrego do not actually say that there was an improvement in the behaviour of the difficult students.

3 It depends on the school; in some schools, many of these initiatives are used successfully.

RLA 9

1 For example: point no. 4 is humanist as Rogers specifically recommends the use of humour in the classroom; point no. 6 is partly based on the behaviourist theory of observational learning – that is, setting a good example for others to imitate; point no. 9 has a cognitive component in that it is encouraging students to develop more internal attributions.

RLA 10

1 The main advantage is that it seemed to encourage student participation in the class. Also, students and teachers enjoyed using it; it created a more informal and democratic atmosphere. Disadvantages included difficulties in keeping it clean, not being able to fit so many students in the room and expense.

2 It is tempting to say that older students, or even young primary school children, would benefit more. It would be interesting to see how effective a soft classroom design would be in a secondary school.

3 Many UK classrooms now have carpets, although few have sofas. Primary school classrooms sometimes have a soft area for story-telling and so on. At sixth form or university level, it is rare to find students sitting in rows of desks.

Chapter 4

RLA 11

1 There is a debate about whether racial harassment is qualitatively different from ordinary bullying. Ordinary bullying tends to be about the individual, whereas the nature of racial harassment is about the group to which that person belongs.

2 Discussion point: Issues should be addressed concerning attitudes to bullying of any students. Sexual harassment might come into this, along with racism and other forms of bullying.

3 Discussion of individual school policies.

RLA 12

1 There are many factors that have influenced the relative achievement of girls and boys. For example, political and economic issues have affected the attitudes of girls to their education. Opportunities for women in employment may have had an effect on attribution and self-esteem. There has been some research recently into the changing attitudes of boys to their education. Peer pressure and conformity can affect their levels of attainment. However, there is some debate as to whether boys are underachieving or whether girls have simply caught up.

2 It is important to discuss social class as one of the main factors in explaining attainment. Some of the reasons why social class is an important factor are: the awareness of what jobs are available when students leave school, cost, attitudes of teachers and attitudes of other students.

RLA 13

1 The obvious answer to this is that the earlier and more straightforward the detection, the better teachers and support staff can help students who have difficulties.

2 The advantages are that this test is quick and easy to administer, and all children can be tested at a relatively early age. The disadvantages are that it cannot identify the specific nature of a student's dyslexia, and further testing needs to be carried out.

RLA 14

1 The advantages of inclusive education include less discrimination, equal access and a more open education system. The disadvantages of inclusive education include cost, issues surrounding how appropriate mainstream education is for students with certain types of learning difficulties and the disadvantages for other children in the class with a child who has special needs.

2 Discussion point: Give your opinions about the relative merits of inclusion and segregation.

RLA 15

1 The risks include bullying by other students, labelling by the teacher and the possibility that students are forced to disguise their ability.

2 Discussion point: Suggestions could include the kind of 'revolving door' policy described in the chapter. Also, the school could promote pro-social values that encourage respect for others, whatever their academic ability.

RLA 16

1 Community assessment identifies certain groups of children who would be overlooked using standard testing.

2 Discussion point: Some people criticize the state education system in the UK for ignoring the needs of gifted children. Parents sometimes set up special Saturday schools, but whether these really meet the needs of gifted children is debatable.

R Selected references

Chapter 1

Bandura, A (1965). 'Influence of models' reinforcement contingencies on the acquisition of imitative responses.' *Journal of Personality and Social Psychology*, 1 (6), pp. 589–95.

Bandura, A (1977). *Social Learning Theory*. Morristown, NJ: General Learning Press.

Bandura, A, Ross, D and Ross, SA (1961). 'Transmission of aggression through imitation of aggressive models.' *Journal of Abnormal and Social Psychology*, 63 (3), pp. 575–82.

Hall, J (1989). 'Chronic psychiatric handicaps.' In Hawton, K, Salkovskis, PM, Kirk, J and Clark, DM (eds) *Cognitive Behaviour Therapy for Psychiatric Problems*. Oxford: Oxford Medical Publications.

Haney, C, Banks, C and Zimbardo, P (1973). 'A study of prisoners and guards in a simulated prison.' *Naval Research Reviews*, 30 (9), pp. 4–17.

Hetherington, EM and Parke, RD (1999). *Child Psychology: A Contemporary Viewpoint*, Boston: McGraw-Hill.

Kegan, R (1994). *In Over Our Heads: The Mental Demands of Modern Life*. Cambridge: Harvard University Press.

Neill, AS (1960). *Summerhill*. New York: Hart.

Piaget, J (1969). *The Mechanisms of Perception*. New York: Basic Books.

Radziszewska, B and Rogoff, B (1988). 'Influence of adult and peer collaborators on the development of children's planning skills.' *Developmental Psychology*, 24, pp. 840–48.

Rogers, CR (1951). *Client-centred Therapy*. Boston: Houghton Mifflin.

Rogers, CR (1961). *On Becoming a Person*. London: Constable.

Rogers, CR (1992). 'The necessary and sufficient conditions of therapeutic personality change.' *Journal of Consulting and Clinical Psychology*, 60 (6), pp. 827–32.

Vygotsky, LS (1962). *Thought and Language*. Cambridge, Mass: MIT Press.

Vygotsky, Lev S (1983). 'School instruction and mental development.' In Donaldson M, Grieve R and Pratt C, *Early Childhood Development and Education*. Oxford: Blackwell.

Wadsworth, BJ (1996). *Piaget's Theory of Cognitive and Affective Development*, London: Longman.

Watson, JB and Rayner, R (1920). 'Conditioned emotional reactions, *Journal of Experimental Psychology*, 3 (1), pp. 1–14.

Chapter 2

Ausubel, DP (1960). 'The use of advance organisers in the learning and retention of meaningful verbal material.' *Journal of Educational Psychology*, 51, pp. 267–72.

Ausubel, DP (1977). 'The facilitation of meaningful verbal learning in the classroom.' *Journal of Educational Psychology*, 12, pp. 162–78.

Bandura, A (1986). *Social foundations of thought and action: a social cognitive theory*. Englewood Cliffs, NJ: Prentice-Hall.

Borich, GD and Tombari, ML (1997). *Educational psychology, A Contemporary Approach*. New York: Longman.

Bruner , JS (1961). *The process of Education*. Cambridge: Mass: Harvard University Press.

Child, D (1997). *Psychology and the Teacher*. London: Cassell.

Gagné, RM (1985). *Conditions of Learning* (4th edition) New York: Holt.

Lepper, MR and Greene, D (1975). 'Turning play into work: effects of adult surveillance and extrinsic rewards on children's intrinsic motivation.' *Journal of Personality and Social Psychology*, 31 (3), pp. 479–86.

Nisbett, RE, Caputo, C, Legant, P and Maracek, J (1973). 'Behaviour as seen by the actor and as seen by the observer.' *Journal of Personality and Social Psychology*, 27 (2), pp. 154–64.

Rosenthal, R and Jacobson, LF (1968). 'Teacher expectations for the disadvantaged.' *Scientific American*, 218 (4), pp. 19–23.

Slatterly, D (1989). *Assessment in Schools*. Oxford: Blackwell.

Slavin, RE (1991). 'Synthesis of research on cooperative learning.' *Educational Leadership*, 48 (5), pp. 71–82.

Tinbergen, N (1952). 'The curious behaviour of the stickleback.' *Scientific American*, 187 (6), pp. 22–6.

Tyler, RW (1974). 'Considerations in selecting objectives.' In Payne, DA (ed.) *Curriculum evaluation: Commentaries on purpose, process, product*. Lexington, MA: DC Heath.

Chapter 3

Bronzaft, AL (1981). 'The effect of a noise abatement program on reading ability.' *Journal of Environmental Psychology*, 1, pp. 215–22.

Cohen, S, Glass, DC and Singer, JE (1973). 'Apartment noise, auditory discrimination and reading ability in children.' *Journal of Experimental Social Psychology*, 9, pp. 407–22.

Cohen, S, Evans, GW, Krantz, DS, Stokols, D and Kelly, S (1981). 'Aircraft noise and children: longitudinal and cross-sectional evidence on adaptation to noise and the effectiveness of noise abatement.' *Journal of Personality and Social Psychology*, 40, pp. 331–45.

Christie, DJ and Glickman, CD (1980). 'The effects of classroom noise on children: evidence for sex differences.' *Psychology in the Schools*, 17, pp. 405–408.

Department for Education and Employment (1999). Circular 10/99 Social Inclusion: Pupil Support. London: DfEE.

Fontana, D (1995). *Psychology for Teachers*. London: Macmillan Press

Gifford, R (1997). *Environmental Psychology*, Needham Heights: Allyn and Bacon.

Hodges, J and Tizard, B (1989). 'Social and family relationships of ex-institutional adolescents.' *Journal of Child Psychology and Psychiatry*, 30 (1), pp. 77–97.

LeFrançois, GR (1997). *Psychology for Teaching* (9th Edition). Belmont: Wadsworth Publishing Company.

Meichenbaum, D and Goodman, J (1971). 'Training impulsive children to talk to themselves: a means of developing self-control.' *Journal of Abnormal Psychology*, 77, pp. 115–126.

Moreno, JM and Torrego, JC (1999). 'Fostering pro-social behaviour in the Spanish school system: a whole school approach.' *Emotional and Behavioural Difficulties*, 4 (2), pp. 23–31.

Mortimore, P, Sammons, P, Stoll, L, Lewis, D and Ecob, R (1988). *School Matters: The Junior Years*. Shepton Mallett: Open Books.

Neill, AS (1960). *Summerhill*. New York: Hart.

Riding, R and Rayner, S (1998). *Cognitive Styles and Learning Strategies*. Trowbridge: Cromwell Press.

Rosenfield, P, Lambert, NM and Black, A (1985). 'Desk arrangements effects on student classroom behavior.' *Journal of Educational Psychology*, 77 (1), pp. 101–108.

Sommner, R and Olsen, H (1980). 'The soft classroom.' *Environment and Behaviour*, 12 (1), pp. 3–16.

Wheldall, K, Morris, M, Vaughan, P and Ng, YY (1981). 'Rows versus tables: an example of the use of behavioural ecology in two classes of eleven-year-old children.' *Educational Psychology*, 1 (2), pp. 171–84.

Zentall, SS (1983). 'Learning environments: a review of physical and temporal factors.' *EEQ: Exceptional Educational Quarterly*, 4, pp. 90–115.

Chapter 4

Bailey, G (1998). 'Medical and psychological models in special needs education 44-60' , in Clark, C, Dyson, D and Millward, A (eds) *Theorising Special Education*. London: Routledge.

Best, L (1993). '"Dragons, dinner ladies and ferrets": sex roles in children's books.' *Sociology Review*, 2 (3), pp. 6–8.

Bernstein, B (1960). 'Language and social class.' *British Journal of Sociology*, 9 (3).

Bourdieu, P (1977). *Outline of a Theory of Practice*. Cambridge: Cambridge University Press.

Bradshaw, J, Clegg, S, and Trayhum, D (1995). 'An investigation into gender bias in educational software used in English primary schools.' *Gender and Education*, 7 (2), pp. 167–74.

Child, D (1997). *Psychology and the Teacher*. London: Cassell.

Clarricoates, K (1987). 'Dinosaurs in the classroom – the "hidden" curriculum in primary schools.' In Arnot, M and Weiner, G (eds) *Gender and the Politics of Schooling*. London: Oxford University Press.

Delmont, S (1990). *Sex Roles and the School*. London: Routledge.

Further Education Funding Council (1998). *Inclusive Learning: Quality Initiative Prospectus*. FEFC.

Freeman, J (1979). *Gifted Children: Their identification and development in a Social Context*. Lancaster: MTP Press.

Gillborn, D and Gipps, C (1996). *Recent Research on the Achievement of Ethnic Minority Students, OFSTED Reviews of Research*. London: HMSO.

Gilroy, P (1990). 'The end of anti-racism.' *New Community*, vol 17, no. 1.

Golombok, S and Fivush, R (1994). *Gender Development*. New York: Cambridge University Press.

Gray, JA and Buffery, AWH (1971). 'Sex differences in emotional and cognitive behaviour in mammals including man: adaptive and neural bases.' *Acta Psychologia*, 35.

Halpern, D (1992). *Sex Differences in Cognitive Abilities*. Hillsdale, New Jersey: Erlbaum.

Hornby, G (1999). 'Inclusion or delusion: can one size fit all?' *Support for Learning*, vol. 14, no. 4.

Hyde JS, Fennema, E and Lamon S J (1990). 'Gender differences in mathematical performance: a meta-analysis.' *Psychological Bulletin*. 107, pp. 135–55.

Judd, J and Borrill, R (1991). 'Parents rush for test books.' In the *Independent on Sunday*, 13 January.

Kidd, R and Hornby, G (1993). 'Transfer from special to mainstream.' *British Journal of Special Education*, 20, pp. 17–19.

Kirby, M *et al* (1997). *Sociology in perspective*. Oxford: Heinemann.

LeFrançois, G (1997). *Psychology for Teaching*. USA: Wadsworth.

Lewis, A (1999). 'Changing views of Special Educational Needs.' *Education 3 to 13*. October 1999.

Lipsky, DK and Gartner, A (1998). 'Taking inclusion into the future.' *Educational Leadership*, 58, pp. 78–81.

Lobban, G (1974). 'Presentation of sex roles in British reading schemes.' *Forum*, 16 (2), pp. 57–60.

Lummis, T and Stevenson, HW (1990). 'Gender differences in beliefs and achievement: a cross-cultural study.' *Developmental Psychology*, 26, pp. 254–63.

Mac An Ghaill, M (1994). *The Making of Men*, Buckingham: Open University Press.

Marston, D (1996). 'A comparison of inclusion only, pull-out only and combined service models for students with mild disabilities.' *Journal of Special Education*, 30, pp. 121–32.

Mirza, H (1992). *Young, Female and Black*. London: Routledge.

Mirza, H (1997). 'Black women in education: a collective movement for social change.' *Black Feminisn: A Reader*. London: Routledge, pp. 270–6.

Newcomb Belcher, R and Fletcher-Carter, R (1999). 'Growing gifted students in the desert. Using alternative, community-based assessment and an enriched curriculum.' *Teaching Exceptional Children*, September/October, 1999.

Pilcher, J (1999). *Women in Contemporary Britain: an Introduction*. London: Routledge.

Renzulli, J Reis, S and Smith, L (1981). *The revolving door identification model*. Mansfield Centre, Conn: Creative Learning Press.

Rist, R (1970). 'Student social class and teacher expectations: the self-fulfilling prophecy in ghetto education.' *Harvard Educational Review*, 40.

Seifert, K (1991). *Educational Psychology*. Boston: Houghton Mifflin Company.

Shore and Kanevsky (1993). 'Thinking processes: being and becoming gifted.' In Heller, K, Monks, F and Passow, A (eds) *International Handbook of Research and Development of Giftedness and Talent*. Oxford: Pergamon.

Stone, M (1981). *The Education of the Black Child in Britain: the Myth of Multiracial Education*. London: Fontana.

Tizard, B and Hughes, M (1986). *Young Children Learning: Talking and Thinking at Home and at School*. London: Fontana.

Trowler, P (1996). *Investigating Education and Training*. London: Collins.

Walkerdine, V (1990). *Schoolgirl Fictions*. London: Verso.

Wright, C (1992). 'Early education: multi-racial primary school classrooms.' In Gill, D, Mayor, B and Blair, M (eds) *Racism and Education: Structures and Strategies*. London: Sage.

Yee, DK and Eccles, JK (1988). 'Parent perceptions and attributions for children's math achievement.' *Sex Roles*, 19, pp. 317–33.

Index